Introvert Explores

Exploring the world one fear at a time.

Victoria Connelly

No part of this publication may be reproduced, distributed, or transmitted in any form or by any means, including photocopying, recording, or other electronic or mechanical methods, without the prior written permission of the publisher.

Some names and locations have been changed for privacy.
Victoria Connelly asserts the moral right to be identified as the author of this work.

Cover design by Jane Dixon Smith
Author photos by Roy Connelly
All other photos copyright © Victoria Connelly

Published by Cuthland Press

ISBN: 978-1-910522-26-4

All rights reserved.
Copyright © 2025 Victoria Connelly

To Aussie Vicki – my solo travelling cheerleader!

'He who is outside his door has the hardest part of
the journey behind him.'
Flemish proverb

The Dreaming Stage

A year ago, something extraordinary happened to me. I went abroad. It might not seem extraordinary in the scheme of things, but the fact that I hadn't left the British Isles for fifteen years made it feel like a pretty big deal.

For the last few years, I've been undergoing a metamorphosis – a strange, menopausal journey where I'm both more fearful than ever and yet more adventurous. I've lost people close to me and my own biological rhythms are clearly telling me that my time here on Earth is finite.

It's time to see a little bit more of the world.

I'm so proud of what I managed to see and do in my first year of travel (which you can read about in my first travel memoir *Introvert Abroad*). I visited three new European cities (Amsterdam, Bruges and Ghent) and three Mediterranean islands (Sicily, Crete and Santorini). The first trip was with a friend, the second was with my brother, the third was with my husband and the fourth was on my own: my first ever solo trip abroad. I'm smiling now just thinking about them. But where should I go this year? And, crucially, could I take all these trips alone?

To warm me up for the year – both physically and mentally – I decide to see the Canary Islands, and Norwich airport has regular flights to Tenerife. This will be my first solo trip of the year and a package holiday. Nice and simple, I hope.

April would be ideal for a trip to Turkey with G Adventures, travelling solo within a small group. It'll be an ideal way to explore a large country and see a lot of sights without the worry of organising it all myself.

In May, I'm hoping to do something very ambitious – flying to Austria and then visiting several cities by train and boat: Vienna, Salzburg, Bratislava and Budapest. I have no idea how well I'll cope with this on my own, but I have an Osprey rucksack now so at least I won't be repeating the embarrassment of rolling my suitcase over endless city cobbles as I did in Bruges.

Then, come September, I'd love to see northern Italy. If my train tour from Austria to Hungary goes well, I'd like to do something similar. It seems wildly exciting when I look at the maps and work out how quickly I can hop from one city to another in this region, but the reality might be utterly exhausting and bewildering. Still, I'd like to give it a go.

Four solo trips in one year. An island in the sun, the ancient ruins of Asia, the jewels of central Europe and the gems of northern Italy. When I think of all the places and the experiences that may lie ahead, it makes me giddy with excitement, but anxiety hijacks me as I make each booking and I worry about all the things that could go wrong from losing my passport to losing my way.

They say that travel broadens the mind but, if you're an introvert, it can also shake the nerves. Still, I have my new mantra to live by and so I fully intend to feel the fear… and travel anyway!

Tenerife – Island of Elements

I'll be honest. Tenerife has never been on any list of mine as a place to visit. Perhaps it's the party island reputation it has. Like Ibiza and Mallorca, Tenerife has become synonymous with the younger holiday crowd with noisy bars serving all-day English breakfasts, beer and cocktails. But these islands existed long before the package holiday and the high-rise hotel, and I'm determined to discover a little of the natural beauty beyond the resorts.

When I realised that I could get to Tenerife from Norwich airport, which is a tiny airport just a ninety-minute drive away, it went straight to the top of my list as a winter destination. I'm not a big fan of winter. I love the frost-bright days when the sky is clear and you can see your dragon-like breath in the crisp air, and I don't much mind the period before Christmas when the nights start to draw in. There's something wonderfully cosy about it all and I love reaching for my beloved winter jumpers, socks and gloves. But it's the weeks in January that start to get me down. The dark, dull weeks after the Christmas lights have been packed away are very trying. The weather worsens, the lawn turns into a muddy sludge, the hens all look bedraggled and I feel I don't see them for nearly long enough because they're all in bed by four o'clock.

I suffer from Raynaud's disease which means the blood flow to my feet and hands is affected by the cold. Sometimes it can look quite startling with the top half of my fingers turning completely white while the bottom half are bright red. It's horribly painful and the warming up process can be excruciating. So winter is definitely not my favourite season.

This winter is made even more trying when our central heating breaks down – for nearly two weeks. And, to make matters worse, we have five named storms in January which rattle the windows of our five-hundred-year-old cottage and creep in under the doors.

No wonder I've been feeling a little sad. Is it the official SAD – Seasonal Affected Disorder? I wouldn't be at all surprised. I'm definitely out of sorts and craving the light. But I know I'm still processing a lot of grief with the loss of both my parents and a dear friend in the past two years. I guess this is the winter of my discontent and, by the middle of January, I'm more than ready to break free from my chrysalis of grief and book my first solo trip abroad this year.

There are some package deals with Love Holidays and I keep an eye on the prices of a three-star hotel in a resort on the south coast of Tenerife. It's a short taxi ride from the airport and I quickly find out that there are boat trips from the port as well as to the neighbouring island of La Gomera. It would be a similar week to my first solo trip in Crete and, as I successfully managed that on my own without any major mishaps, I feel confident that I can cope with Tenerife.

After dithering for about a week, I finally make my booking. It seems like an eye-watering price for a week in a three-star hotel, but I guess they can pretty much charge what they like and us Brits, desperate to escape the cold, grey days of winter, will happily pay it and at least my flights are included and breakfast too.

And then the fun bit of the trip begins as I find out more about my destination. The centre of the island is dominated by Teide National Park and the volcano, Mount Teide, which sits at its heart and – like Etna on Sicily which I visited last year – there's a chance to ascend by cable car. I'll also be able to book a day trip to the unspoilt island of La Gomera, famous for its ancient laurel forest and dramatic landscape. There are countless boat trips to see whales and dolphins from the port where I'll be staying and there might even be an opportunity to go paragliding between the mountains and the coast.

A volcano. An island. The sea. Paragliding. Fire, earth, water and air. It seems like I'm about to fully embrace the four elements this winter.

Fire

As I'm not hiring a car, I start my first day in Tenerife by finding a tour operator to help me arrange my week. There's a company called First Excursions and they're easy to find on the seafront at Los Cristianos – their huge colourful posters advertising the very best that Tenerife has to offer. I'm greeted by Mark from Manchester. He's been working in Tenerife for seven years and loves the fact that he can go to work in a T-shirt.

We sit down at the back of the kiosk and I get out my notebook, letting him know the trips I'd like to do, and the first thing I'm keen to see is Teide National Park to take the cable car up the volcano. So we book that as my first day trip. It's an exciting start and the good news is that the coach pickup is right outside my hotel. Indeed, all the trips I book leave from my hotel so I don't have the mad scramble to get into town early in the morning like I did in Crete.

One thing that does hit me though is a case of nerves the next morning when I wake up at five. My pickup isn't until 9.25 a.m. so I try and rest as much as I can, but I can't easily switch off my anxiety. I haven't had a headache for a few weeks now and I'm paranoid about getting one while away – especially in this hotel which is very noisy. It would be impossible to rest well here. But, somehow, I manage a little more sleep before I get up for an early breakfast.

When I return to my room, I turn to my two portable travelling companions to restore a semblance of calm and do some yoga on my travel mat and listen to some Eckhart Tolle on my phone. It helps a little, but there's still a nervous energy coursing through me as I leave the hotel and make my way to the bus stop. There's quite a crowd and I quickly realise that we're all waiting for different coaches to take us on different adventures and, when a coach pulls up, everyone surges forward, fearful of missing their trip because there's no indication where it's going. This happens several times before my coach appears. A courier with a clipboard ticks my name off a list and I climb on board. It's a nice coach and I choose a seat towards the back on the left. It's not too crowded so I have plenty of room to myself.

We leave the bright bustle of Los Cristianos and it isn't long before we turn off the main road and start to ascend through beautiful pine forests and there's a bit of excitement when we slow down to pass the Pino Gordo or 'Fat Pine'. It's the oldest pine on Tenerife, estimated to be around seven or eight hundred years old. Frustratingly, we can only see a fraction of this colossus from the coach, but how lovely to see this guardian of the island.

Our guide points out almond trees which are in blossom, but this landscape belongs to the pine tree and we're told how resilient it is as it's fire-resistant and can resprout after losing its needles in a fire, so it's the perfect inhabitant for a volcanic island.

When we leave the treeline behind, the landscape opens up and I feel like we're entering another realm altogether. The earth seems bare and raw and has thrown up strange sculpture-like shapes against the vivid blue sky. There are several stops to allow us to wander a little to take photos of this fantastical place. Our guide leads the way on one of the stops, taking us to see the mysterious rock formation that's shaped like Cinderella's shoe or a seahorse – I suppose depending on which way you're looking at it – and it really is extraordinary. She also picks up a large rock that has been hidden under another one and I see black striations of obsidian glistening in the sun. It is stunning. I would love a piece but we've already been warned that taking any rock from Teide – big or small – could result in a four hundred euro fine if caught. I take a photo instead.

We have only walked a short distance from the coach but, when I glance back, the vehicle looks absolutely tiny in the vastness of the landscape. It makes me realise how small and vulnerable we are in this place and also how lucky we are to be here seeing it all. I'm so struck by the colours around me. At first glance, it might seem a bleak and barren place but the earth is a tapestry of pale pinks, silvery greens and rich ochres.

We can see the top of Mount Teide now. This will be the third volcano I have ascended. The most recent one was Etna on Sicily and, although my brother and I chose a bright sunny day in June to visit, it was shrouded in cloud which, despite being very atmospheric as we went up in our little cable car, meant you couldn't see a thing from the top. But today, looking out of the coach window, we can clearly see the top of Teide.

At over three thousand seven hundred metres, Mount Teide is the highest point on Spanish soil and is the world's third highest volcano after Mauna Loa and Mauna Kea in Hawaii. It is an active volcano although it last erupted in 1909. Depending what you read, it erupts

roughly every fifty to one hundred years so it's definitely due, but I try not to think about that as we reach the car park.

It's a little chaotic as we leave the coach. We're given three different times to memorise. Luckily, the coach driver has written these on a little white board and I take a photo to have it handy on my phone. The first time is for the cable car up. The second is for the cable car down. And the third is the time to meet the coach. We are warned that it is a *very* long bus ride back from Teide if we miss our coach, or a *very* expensive taxi ride.

I get a fantastic spot in the cable car on the way up and watch as the car park recedes. There are thirty to forty of us crammed together for this adventure and there's a nervous woman near me who bursts into laughter every time the cable car goes over a support tower and judders a little. She simply can't control herself. It makes a few of us laugh too.

The journey up the flank of Teide lasts eight minutes and we've been advised to rest for a good five minutes once at the top to acclimatise. It's a good excuse to simply stand and look at the views. I put my coat on but it's not as cold or windy as I imagined it would be and I soon take it off again.

Once I feel acclimatised, I walk along the path into the lunar landscape. The air becomes increasingly sulphurous which makes me smile. It is by no means a pleasant smell, but what an experience to inhale a living, breathing volcano. There aren't many people here and the few that are soon overtake me. I decide to double back to sit on a rock and just soak up the atmosphere. It's so quiet. Quieter than anything I've experienced on the island so far and it's wonderful. I'm sitting in a place where some pretty scary volcanic activity has happened in the past and yet it's one of the most peaceful places I've ever been. The sun is warm on my face and arms and I'd love to spend more time here, but I'm aware that we have been given a strict timetable and mustn't miss our coach's departure so I make my way back to the cable car.

A writer friend of mine loves Tenerife and has visited every year for the last eight years, staying in one of the busy resorts on the south coast. When I send her a photo of me at the top of Teide, she says she's never been. I guess everybody's trips are different and I quickly learn that a lot of people remain in their resorts, eating, drinking and simply soaking up the sun. Indeed, one of the first people I speak to at my resort has absolutely nothing planned for her time in Tenerife. That might be a good way to relax, of course, but it does seem a shame to me to miss out on the raw wilderness of this island and I'm so glad that I've seen a bit of it today.

Earth

It's my third day in Tenerife and I'm about to take the ferry to the neighbouring island of La Gomera. I've joined a coach tour and our guide is a young man from Sicily called Andreas, and he seems to have singled me out because I'm the only solo.

'Come with me,' he says, leading me onto the coach. 'You are with the Italian family.'

And there they are – a rather large man sitting with his legs splayed out into the seat Andreas tells me is mine. On the opposite side of the aisle are his wife and daughter. Only the daughter speaks a little English.

'Do not change seats,' Andreas goes on. 'Remember where you are sitting otherwise it will confuse everything.'

I nod. Message understood. I squash myself into the seat next to the large Italian man. The family talks across me and I can only understand the occasional word. As the man shifts himself awkwardly, I imagine his wife has just told him to give me more room. I offer to swap seats but he shakes his head. To my mind, it would be much easier for me to be next to the window and for him to take the aisle seat where he'd have more leg room and the family wouldn't need to talk over me. But it's a short ride to the port for the ferry so I don't think too much about it.

The other thing Andreas presses home is the importance of having our passports ready as we will need them for getting on the ferry – both ways. It's rather exciting and something that certainly doesn't happen in the UK when you visit say – the Isle of Wight.

As I queue, passport and ticket in hand, I glance up at the ferry and nearly freak out at the large patches of chipped metalwork on the side of the boat until I realise that they aren't chips – they're images of the islands of Tenerife and La Gomera. Panic averted.

Andreas has told us to look out for dolphins on the one-hour crossing as they can often be seen in the wake at the back of the ferry. This is all the encouragement I need to take up position there, pulling my hat down firmly and hugging the rails, my phone safe in its waterproof pouch around my neck. And I am rewarded about twenty minutes into the short journey with a sighting of two or three dolphins to the right of the foamy, white wake. It's a brief delight but so worth watching the waves for.

As we near the end of the journey, I venture inside the ferry and cross to the front, eager for my first glimpse of La Gomera. It's the second smallest of the Canary Islands and is far less developed than Tenerife. It's famous for its rugged landscape, dense forests and mountain trails which are popular with hikers. I can't wait to see it.

I'm the first one of my coach 'family' onto the vehicle and I take the initiative, sitting in the window seat. I hope this doesn't make me seem cheeky, but it strikes me as the most practical way of doing things. Sure enough, the Italian family don't seem to mind. The father takes the window seat on the other side of the aisle and the daughter sits next to me. I'll make sure to offer her the window seat at some point – maybe after lunch – as I would hate to be thought a window hog.

After leaving the port, we twist ever upwards into the mountains of La Gomera. Andreas is a wonderful guide. He does his commentary first in English, then French, then Italian. The trouble is, those whose language he isn't speaking at any given time, start up conversations of their own, making it hard to hear him. Luckily, he is onto this and, like a stern teacher, asks for a little respect – in three languages.

Like Tenerife, La Gomera is an island of two halves with the northern half being a lot lusher than the south, and this is marked by one particular tunnel which slices through a mountain. Andreas is so excited to show us the north side that there's an air of expectant anticipation as we enter the tunnel, wondering what will greet us when we see the light again. In all fairness, we still see the cactus-scattered hills that we left behind on the other side, but it isn't long before the landscape becomes a little greener.

We soon enter the Hermigua valley. Meteorologists have claimed that it has the most perfect climate as it's never below fifteen Celsius or above twenty-seven. I have to say, I find that very appealing indeed. And it's so lush. There are bananas, aloe vera and avocados growing in profusion as well as many other crops on the terraced landscape. The views down the precipitous slopes to the coast are jaw-droppingly beautiful too, although Andreas has one or two minor fits after we stop and several of his charges weave across the dangerous bends of the road in order to take the perfect photo.

As we enter a small town, our coach driver slows down and goes round a small roundabout a second time to allow us to see bananas being packed up for export. It's an amusing moment with a lot of us taking photos from the windows. This must be a very average sort of job here on La Gomera, but it's a remarkable sight for those of us who only ever see bananas in neat bunches with a sticky label on them sitting on a supermarket shelf.

Our lunch stop is at a hilltop restaurant. The views are straight down into a steep valley and Andreas advises us to venture downstairs to the toilets even if we don't need to go because the view is worth it. And he's right. There's a covered walkway and there are palm trees, banana trees and pink rose-like flowers. There's also a wonderful dragon tree and the landscape has been terraced for food production.

When I go back upstairs to the restaurant, I find I'm the last one to join our group and that all the seats are taken around the tables. I try not to panic and find Andreas and he quickly places me on a table by myself, telling me more people will join soon from another coach. In the meantime, a waitress approaches me with watercress soup.

'Where's your husband?' she asks.

I'm a little surprised by her bluntness and part of me wants to tell her that he's at home working his way through a long list of chores I've left him to do. I think of Shirley Valentine sitting on her own in her Greek hotel, loving the peace and a chance to simply be her.

One thing being alone at the table allows me to do is observe. The view from the restaurant is stunning and I glance down into the valley and see a man in the distance walking around a terraced garden. There are trees and vegetables and I love getting this little glimpse into a life being led in this extraordinary landscape.

After finishing my starter, the other promised coach arrives and I am joined by two German couples who speak wonderful English and it's fun to ask about their travels. One of the couples is just six months away from retiring and has a trip around the world planned. I try to imagine what that must be like – to plan a lengthy trip encompassing the whole world.

After lunch, we are treated to a demonstration of La Gomera's famous whistling language – *el silbo* – used in the hills and valleys of the island to communicate over vast distances. It is still taught in schools today and Andreas gives our demonstrator some phrases and names to translate into whistles.

Leaving our whistling waitress, we make our way to our next stop on the tour: a small garden filled with exotic trees and flowers. I spot a pink flower the size of a dinner plate. Its centre looks spiky and its outer petals are a few shades darker. When I look it up, I see it's a protea. It's certainly not anything I've come across before and I'm dazzled by it. The trees here are also mesmerising. Many are covered in thick moss and look positively furry.

The coach climbs further up La Gomera and we soon enter the ancient laurel woods, the sunlight filtering through the trees. It is a beautiful scene, but it's then that my worst nightmare happens and a headache strikes. I feel drained pretty quickly and, when the coach stops for a tour of the woods, I wonder how I'm going to cope. There's a brief talk before we're given some time to either walk among the trees or have a drink and something to eat. I walk along the path into the wood, hoping to find a quiet place away from everyone so I can take some tablets. I feel pretty anxious that things might spiral quickly as I know we have many more hours before the tour ends. Then there's the hour back on the ferry and getting back to my hotel. I try not to worry about it. I just need to take one step at a time – quite literally – for I'm even finding that an effort now and actually find myself walking with my eyes closed which isn't ideal.

It's so frustrating to feel this way in this beautiful place but I'm not surprised. The lethal cocktail of my recently disturbed sleep, the disruption in my normal routine, the rather meagre lunch today and the twisty and noisy journey on the coach seem to have melded and collided in my head. I'm struggling and I'm fearful of being on my own in case things get worse.

The tour continues and our next stop is the Roque de Agando – one of the most iconic viewpoints on the island. I've been looking forward to seeing this and the view into the tree-covered valley doesn't disappoint and takes my mind off how I'm feeling for a few minutes. It looks like something out of Jurassic Park and I half-expect to see a dinosaur at any moment.

We finally arrive in La Gomera's delightful capital, San Sebastian. It's the size of a modest town with some lovely old buildings and a beautiful park. By this stage, I'm quite desperate to break away from the coach tour and find a bench in a quiet corner somewhere, but Andreas refuses to tell us the time of the ferry departure until he's

given us his spiel and he marches us through town, pointing out a few sights along the way.

This is the town from where Christopher Columbus departed before discovering the Americas, having stopped at the island to restock. It's believed he had a rather intense love affair while here, but that's the last thing I want to hear about today.

Finally, Andreas gives us directions to the ferry, but he still doesn't tell us the actual departure time. Instead, he tells us that we must be on board by five fifteen. I'm guessing that, if he told us when the ferry actually leaves, people would push their luck and risk being late. It's obviously happened before and I admire his stealth.

When we all disperse, I pop into a little shop to buy a snack.

'Hola!' I say, sounding a lot brighter than I feel as I approach the counter. The man serving smiles and tells me the price – in perfect English.

'How did you know I was English?' I ask. 'It's the hat, isn't it?'

We laugh as I wonder what it was about that one simple Spanish word I attempted which gave me away.

I make my way to a square full of glorious laurel trees. Their white trunks are gnarled and knobbly and they make beautiful companions for my last few minutes on the island. There's a café under the trees and a few benches where tourists sit yet it's peaceful and perfect.

It's been a long and draining day but La Gomera has bewitched me and I'm longing to return already and explore at a more leisurely pace. I'd love to discover the footpaths into those lush valleys, to sit under its trees, to feel the sun on its rocks. It feels like an undiscovered gem of an island compared to its bigger, bustling sister island of Tenerife and I know it's stolen a little of my heart.

Water

I love islands. Large ones, small ones, rocky ones, sandy ones – I think it's knowing that I'm never too far from the sea that I find really appealing because the sea means boat trips and boat trips mean wildlife.

When my brother and I visited Sicily last summer, one of the highlights was a boat trip from Giardini Naxos where we saw dolphins. It was my first sighting of them in the wild and it was the most magical experience. And I can't wait to see what lives in the waters off Tenerife's coast so I book one of the local boats that leaves Los Cristianos three times a day for a two-hour trip to see the resident dolphins and pilot whales in the waters between Tenerife and La Gomera.

It's quite a walk from the booking office to the port and I have just a few minutes to get there, weaving my way through the lunchtime pedestrians. I can see a small crowd waiting for the boat trip when I arrive so I'm glad not to have missed it. The gates to the dock are closed and there doesn't seem to be anything happening. A young man then approaches me and another lady standing close by.

'Have you booked the two-thirty?' he asks. 'It's been cancelled.'

I shake my head. 'I just booked it about fifteen minutes ago. I don't think it's cancelled.'

He holds his phone out. He's booked via the GetYourGuide app and a contact has just rung him to say it's definitely cancelled. The other woman standing nearby is on the three o'clock boat with another company.

'Come on mine. It's leaving now,' she says as the gates are opened and a man appears. Everyone surges forward but the man holds his hands up.

'It's pretty rough out there today,' he says. 'If you need to cancel, do so now.'

This puts me in a quandary. There aren't many slots in my week when I'll be able to do this trip again.

'There's less chance of seeing the dolphins and whales,' he adds. This makes my mind up for me. There's no point risking feeling queasy *and* not seeing the wildlife. So I get a refund on my ticket, hoping I'll be able to squeeze the local boat trip in on another day.

It's funny how things work out. On my way back from the day trip to Mount Teide, I decided that I simply couldn't do another long day purely on a coach. The twisty Tenerife roads and the endless stopping and starting for dropping people off at their hotels is utterly draining. So I rang Mark, my booking agent at First Excursions, to cancel a trip which would have taken me even further than Teide. When I popped by the shop for my refund, I decided to book a trip on *Freebird* – a catamaran which leaves from Porto Colón just up the coast from where I'm staying. Relief surged through me that I'd exchanged another potentially hot and uncomfortable day on a coach for a trip out to sea and a chance to see wildlife instead.

The thing is, and I'll be totally honest here, I'm always surprised by how popular things are. When I pictured the catamaran, I imagined maybe eight or nine other people on board with me. But there are two coachloads of us queuing at the port on the morning of the trip and it seems that we're all being crammed onto the same catamaran. Luckily, there is plenty of room, but there is a mad scramble for the loungers at the front. I'm content with a bench at the side of the boat; it's close to the rails for spotting any wildlife out at sea.

After a few minutes of 'party boat' atmosphere with music at a volume to scare away any introvert let alone a sea creature, things become a little quieter and it isn't long before we spot the pilot whales. It's my first sighting of them. They're strikingly similar to dolphins at first glance although darker skinned and larger, with wonderfully rounded heads which we get a good view of as two come very close to the boat. I get some video although cut away just as one surfaces as another is swimming right towards me. I truly don't know where to look – the sea seems alive with them. Even more exciting is when I overhear the commentary from another boat nearby. Apparently, we've just seen baby pilot whales and that's rare so we're very lucky indeed.

The catamaran drops anchor close to land and there's a chance for swimming. I've decided not to as we're still very much out at sea here and I do like to know that I can put my feet down and find land if I need to, but I watch as other intrepid souls leap from the boat into the inky-blue depths. The captain is watching like an anxious parent and has warned people that there are jellyfish – he has actually spotted one – and they will sting if contact is made, but it doesn't seem to be putting people off.

When it's time to head back to shore, there's that sad feeling of leaving the sea and its creatures behind. But I promise to return soon.

In fact, it's the very next day when I get a chance to go out on the *Bahriyeli* – the boat from Los Cristianos which was cancelled on my first day in Tenerife. We're warned that it is a little rocky out at sea but the sun is shining and I'm determined not to miss this chance.

I sit at the front and a member of the crew tells us that it's less rocky at the back of the boat, but the sun is full on me here and there are only three others around me. It feels bright, spacious and a little daring; I'm willing to give it a go, although a part of me is thinking about the time my husband Roy and I took a boat trip to Fingal's Cave, Staffa off the Scottish coast and I felt horribly seasick. Have I grown sea legs since? I guess I'm about to find out.

I quickly message Roy to let him know what I'm doing in case anything untoward happens. He messages back: *Keep your eyes on the horizon.*

They weren't kidding about it being rocky. The horizon dips and rises alarmingly. It's a bit splashy too at the front and the woman sitting nearest the prow almost loses the cup of coffee she's brought on board. She doesn't seem to be coping and a member of the crew approaches to escort her to the back where the motion shouldn't affect her so much. But, surprisingly, I'm feeling okay. In fact, I'm positively enjoying it – the sound of the water, the salt spray in the air – the occasional splash on my face. It's all so invigorating.

Unfortunately, there doesn't seem to be any wildlife and we're an hour into our two-hour trip. The boat is now heading back towards shore and I feel a little sad that we might have missed our chance to see something. But then the captain announces that we're heading towards the fish farm near the cliffs in the hope of spotting dolphins who are often seen taking an easy meal there, and we do spot a few but they're such a long way off that I'm not really sure if I've seen them or not. A member of the crew is standing near me as I watch and he points to something in the distance, declaring it to be a turtle. Oh, how I wish I had binoculars. And then, closer to the boat in the other direction, I see a turtle floating on the waves. It's a little way off but the shape is unmistakable. It is wonderful – a magical moment that I'll never forget. My first turtle!

I get off the boat, a huge smile on my face even though I still feel as if I'm rocking. A member of the team opens the gate from the dock area for us and I thank her, blurting out like an excited child that I've just seen my first turtle. She acknowledges how rocky it's been today and offers me a discounted price on a future boat trip if I want to try again. *If!*

I just hope that I get the opportunity.

***

The sky is bright with light clouds when I get the chance to board the *Bahriyeli* again. The sea is a little rocky, but less so than my previous trip. This time, I sit upstairs, aiming to get a different perspective on things. I'm sitting next to a woman from South Africa and her partner. They've been travelling for a while now and have been to Egypt and the Maldives. It makes my little trip to Tenerife seem positively tame and I wonder if I'll have the courage to go further afield in the future.

It's still pretty rocky on the water and when I get up to record a video, I fall backwards onto the South African lady. But that's okay because she crashed into me just minutes before when she attempted to stand up.

Once again, we spend an hour with nothing much happening at all. I try not to feel disappointed as I know this is my last boat trip in Tenerife. And then it happens. Dolphins!

There are six or seven of them between our boat and another and we watch them for what seems like an age. It is absolutely riveting. Everyone on board is watching in awe as the dolphins break the surface over and over again, the sun turning their curved backs silver. At one point, they are so close to the boat that you can see them under the waves just before they surface. It's a glimpse of another world and how beautiful it is.

After the dolphins leave us, one of the young crew members gives us a talk about these beautiful animals and how important conservation work is. We hear of the awful annual massacre of dolphins in Japan and the sad fact that a dolphin lives for just fifteen years in captivity when it can reach fifty years in the wild. He doesn't specifically mention the famous Tenerife tourist attraction where both dolphins and orcas are trained to perform but the message is very clear. These animals belong in the wild and, if we want to see them, it should be on their terms.

When the boat trip is over, I haven't quite had my fill of the sea and I realise that this is my last chance to swim here and I'm going to take it. It's a little cloudy and a lot cooler than it has been, but it's still a good deal warmer than any day we could have in the UK at this time of year and I'm determined to swim.

I find myself a little patch of beach and disrobe. I'm already wearing my bikini but lay out my microfibre towel and pop on my swim shoes. I watch as an elderly couple cross the beach and walk towards the sea together. They're holding hands. She looks a little unsteady, but there is no hesitation and they walk straight into the water. This gives me the confidence boost I need. I have no excuses.

Of course, it's easier said than done and, as I take my turn, I do it incrementally, the waist to shoulders section always being the hardest to submerge. But what a joy once I'm in and floating.

A young man follows me in. He's holding a can of drink, wades in up to his waist and then plops down on his back like a sea otter, opening his can and swigging from it.

I float around for a while, doing a full three-hundred-and-sixty-degree turn, taking in the beach, the rows of restaurants, my hotel in the distance and then the open water and the little port where the boat I've just been on is now docked for the night. There are three young boys playing with a ball on the shore and, every so often, they enter the water just to splash about a bit. But it's quiet at this end of the beach. I have found a moment of calm and a space of my own.

Air

When you think of the Canary Islands, you think of perfect weather. At least, that's what I'd imagined for my winter trip. But the Canary Islands can get very windy. Indeed, the name of one of the islands – Fuerteventura – is thought to mean 'strong winds'. The boat trips I've been on from Los Cristianos prove just how windy it can get and it looks like something else I've booked might now be in jeopardy.

I watch the wind tossing the palm tree beside my hotel balcony, its enormous fronds dancing in a frenzy. If they don't allow the boats to go out when it's too windy, they're certainly not going to let us jump off a mountain and paraglide, are they?

I listen to the wind all evening and into the night. I'm awake early and it's still windy at six in the morning. I'm not being picked up until after nine so there is still time for the wind to blow itself out. It's a little calmer and I don't want to give up hope just yet. Today is my one chance to do this; I don't have any more time on the island.

By eight o'clock the wind has definitely died down and I check my phone to make sure that nothing has been cancelled by the company, Fly Tenerife. There is no message. I *think* I'm going to fly this morning!

I'm being picked up outside my hotel and a black minibus arrives bang on time. I'm the first in and chat to the young driver. He's not an instructor but he has done a few flights.

We pick up a family of three in Costa Adeje. The mother, Amy, and her husband and teenage son are from Wrexham in Wales. Amy asks if I'm on my own and when I tell her I am, she says, 'Well, you're with us now.' I smile. If ever there was a time this week when I needed some company, it's now!

The minibus leaves the coastal resorts and winds its way up a mountainside. But, rather bizarrely, we stop at a McDonald's which seems to be in the middle of nowhere. There's a group of guys waiting for us – our instructors – and a few other people who are to paraglide with us. Amy and I rush into the McDonald's. It's our only chance to use a toilet. We then jump on board another minibus and head even higher into the hills. At this point, we could be going anywhere. We might have been kidnapped and are now being taken to some remote location where nobody will ever find us again.

But – no – we soon park and are told to leave everything on the bus. This makes me intensely anxious. I've not been parted from my money belt all week – I've even been sleeping with it under my pillow. But there's no room for negotiation here. The only thing we're allowed to take is glasses.

As we leave the minibus someone is shouting instructions. The most important thing to remember is to keep moving forward. You must *not* sit down. Your instructor will tell you when to sit. I try and commit this to memory. I do not want to let myself down, cause an accident or not be able to launch.

I'm introduced to my instructor Orlando. He's from Cuba and seems like an amiable chap. His son is also an instructor and is here today. We all walk to the launch site together – a rather scruffy slope covered in Astroturf. We have a little time to wait while Orlando contacts the team down on the coast. They have to make sure the conditions are safe. It might seem perfect up here in the mountains, but it might be completely different down by the sea which is where we're heading.

One of the instructors tells us that they're watching the darker waves on the sea, assessing which way they're moving. The wind is everything. It's a fascinating world we're seeing but the waiting gives me plenty of time to get nervous.

I chat to Amy and we watch as a couple of the instructors start to kit out the younger children. How brave they are! There's a mum waiting with us. She's launching three of her kids but not doing it herself. She nods towards her daughter.

'She's killing herself for Instagram,' she says, telling us of all the adventures they've had during the last few days and how very expensive it is when you're a family.

'We went on a boat trip – cost over a hundred pounds.'

I do feel for them. As a solo traveller, I only have myself to think of. It certainly keeps the cost down.

I watch as a couple of the kids take off first including the Instagram girl. But she's having problems and fails to get off the ground. Her mother shouts encouragement to her, repeating what her instructor is telling her and, finally, she's off.

Orlando approaches me. It looks like we're going next. He gives me the instructions again as he puts me into my harness and gives me a helmet. I ask if I have an emergency parachute. No, I don't. He tells me that only he does and we're strapped together. I try not to think about a drama series I watched recently where the pilot of a small plane had a heart attack and crashed. Orlando looks pretty fit to me and the paragliding only lasts twenty minutes. Nothing is going to happen in that time. *Don't think about being helpless in the air at a thousand metres.*

Orlando gives me the GoPro camera on the end of a long black stick. It's connected by a cable and I'm concerned that I'm going to trip over it while trying to launch. I didn't realise there'd be this other dimension to worry about, but it will be good to have photos, I have to admit – just to prove to myself and Roy that I really did do it. Because I am going to do this. I'm all strapped up. We've been given the go-ahead and we're just waiting for our turn.

I ask Orlando about landing and he says you simply put your legs out and one or two steps is all you'll need to take. It seems wonderfully simple compared to the take-off so I refocus on the here and now.

There's a windsock at the bottom left of the slope we're standing on. I'm to walk towards it and then start running. I am NOT to sit down. If I feel the chute tugging behind me, I'm not to turn. I'm to keep moving towards the windsock. And I'm NOT to sit down.

'Right!' I say, my eyes never leaving the windsock. What on earth am I doing here? Although the *on earth* part of that question reminds me that I'm about to leave it at any moment – unless I make the mistake of sitting down!

Then suddenly, Orlando says, 'One, two, three, walkingwalkingwalking!' And we're moving. I feel an enormous tug from behind like he warned me, but I keep moving forward.

'Run, run! Okay!' he cries.

We're off – and *up*.

I give a whoop of delight and laugh, and Orlando pulls me back into the seat that I didn't dare sit on until instructed. I did it! I walked. I ran. I did NOT sit down until told. And now I'm airborne and the land is far beneath me and the mountains are behind me and it's incredible. Orlando positions my left hand so I'm holding the strap and takes the GoPro from me so that I can hold on with my right hand too.

'Yeah!' he cries and I laugh again. 'Woo hoo!'

One of the first things I notice straightaway is the noise as we move through the air. I had no idea it would be so noisy. Is it this

loud for birds when they fly? It always looks so peaceful when I'm watching them from the ground.

Orlando holds the camera to our right. 'Say hello to camera! *Yee-ha!*'

I laugh. I didn't think I'd be laughing so much. Is it nervous laughter? Probably a little. But this is incredible. I've always wanted to fly – to experience moving through the air. Whenever you are asked which superpower you'd want – say, for example, superhuman strength or invisibility, I always choose the ability to fly. And now I am. High above Tenerife, leaving the mountains and heading for the coast, the island of La Gomera clear across the sea.

We cross a main road and Orlando points out some banana plantations. There are some pretty houses here and we come alarmingly close to a hotel and pool. I wonder what the guests there make of us all falling out of the sky. It must be a little unnerving as you try to relax by the pool.

'Remind me of the legs again,' I say as we swoop left and right, ever-descending. This is the moment I've been most nervous about but he merely tells me to put my legs out. We're heading towards a sandy car park and those that launched before me are already down on the ground. How Orlando manages to find a space between them safely, I do not know.

'Legs up!' he calls to me. I'm holding the GoPro so that he can manoeuvre us and we land safely. I laugh and he grabs onto me to steady me.

'Stand up!' he says as I almost collapse to the ground.

'Okay? How was it – good?'

'It was amazing!' I say, still laughing.

He unhooks me and I thank him, telling him that it's a very special thing to have done on my last day in Tenerife. He grins and tells me that everybody seems to wait until the last day of their holiday to go paragliding in case something goes wrong. I hadn't even thought about that.

It seems strange to simply walk away from him after sharing something so incredible. I wonder how many times a week he does this – how many people he gives this gift of flight to. But I'm also grateful to myself for gifting me this experience. When I saw that it was an option on Tenerife, I thought it would be the perfect place for it with its mountains and its coast. It's certainly been the most amazing way to end my trip to this magical island.

Adios, Tenerife!

My alarm clock has never failed me and yet that doesn't stop me from not trusting it on the morning of departure and I awake hideously early. I'm unable to get to sleep again so give myself up to the travel day ahead.

I've checked that the hotel can book me a taxi to the airport on my morning of departure and, when I check out at seven o'clock, they make a call for me and a taxi arrives within two minutes. I've recently watched a vlog about taxis and the advice is to set the price – or at least ask it – before getting in or handing your luggage to the driver. So, when the driver goes to grab my suitcase, I quickly ask what the fare will be. I don't want any nasty surprises or to be taken advantage of as a solo female traveller.

It's Sunday morning and the roads are quiet and we're at the airport in about fifteen minutes. I whizz through security and, when I check the departure board, I see that the gate for my flight won't be announced for about ninety minutes. Well, at least I'm here in plenty of time and have successfully negotiated the first part of my journey home.

I have a moment of pride looking up at the destinations on the departure board with locations like Paris and Milan and then – amongst all the great cities of the world – my little home town, Norwich.

I've loved my time in Tenerife. As I wait at the airport, I think back over the week I've spent here. I've seen so many stunning landscapes from Teide National Park to the ancient woods and valleys of La Gomera, and I've watched dolphins, whales and even a turtle out at sea. But there have been some smaller moments too which have been equally memorable. One of my favourite things was simply wandering around on my own – whether that was following the rocky path on Mount Teide and experiencing those silent few minutes on the slopes of the volcano or exploring the streets of Los Cristianos at night, watching fellow holidaymakers parading along the front in their finery. It's still such a surprise to me that I can just do this sort of thing on my own now. It feels a little like I'm gate-crashing a really fabulous party.

There was one evening where I found myself at the church in the centre of Los Cristianos. I'd been hoping to peep inside but it had always looked closed. Then, on my penultimate evening, I saw somebody entering through a side door and decided to try again. I walked straight into a holy communion service. Almost immediately, a woman approached me with a collection plate and, rather flustered, I had to scramble in my bag for my ripper wallet which made the most awful noise as I opened it. Once I'd managed to recover after that embarrassment, the service was a beautiful experience, even though I couldn't understand the language. The singing was very moving and I had a lovely surprise when the congregation were invited to greet their neighbours and a stranger behind me approached to shake my hand. It was one of those moments that you stumble into quite accidentally but which will leave their impression on you forever.

What I discovered very quickly on this trip was that I like being warm. I am not a fan of British winters which go on for far too long. I miss the light and I miss the feel of sunshine on my skin. Being outdoors is a gift to me and I adored being able to walk around – even once darkness had fallen – and feel warm – in February! My evening walks through town, sitting under the flamboyant trees, were delicious and may well become a new winter routine. I saw swifts while I was in Tenerife. Were they our swifts from the summer months? They definitely have the right idea – flying south for the winter and I think I'd do well to emulate them.

I knew I'd struggle with the largeness of the hotel. I found it very noisy and being on the first floor meant that I could hear the entertainment each evening. Luckily, my noise-cancelling headphones saved my sanity and enabled me to rest and recharge at the end of each day.

But I give myself credit for having coped with another solo trip. I still suffered from the same nerves as I had in Crete and maybe that will never leave me as an introvert. Simply leaving my hotel room to face the day took enormous courage, but I did it. And I still had all the same fears about being in a foreign country alone – my fear of getting ill, of having an accident, of getting lost or losing my passport. I did my best to mitigate those fears: taking all my medications with me, holding onto hand rails on ferries and coaches, making sure I always knew roughly where I was going and keeping in touch with Roy via the location finder on WhatsApp, and wearing my money belt – even going as far as to take it into the bathroom with me in my hotel and sleeping with it under my pillow. And, for the most part, I was so caught up with experiencing this glorious new place that I honestly didn't have time to think about being nervous because I was truly living in the present moment. There were a couple of slightly uncomfortable, 'Where's your husband?' questions fired at me, but it wasn't anything I couldn't cope with.

One thing I was very aware of was that I could so easily fall into a cocoon-like routine when travelling solo. My trip to Tenerife felt very similar to my first to Crete. They were both sunny islands where I booked hotels close to the airport. I also found tour operators on my first full days and entrusted them with my week, planning only the occasional thing to do under my own steam. I have forgiven myself for still being such a baby traveller. I'm learning my way around the world and finding out what I'm capable of. But I'm going to shake things up a bit for my next two trips this year.

Something I'm quickly learning about this travel business is that, rather than sating my appetite, it is merely whetting it for I'm not so much ticking places off my list as adding to them. I'm already planning to come back to Tenerife and explore the north of the island. I'd also love to see more of La Gomera as well as visit neighbouring La Palma and Gran Canaria.

My plane leaves on time and there is the most spectacular view of Mount Teide from the air. Its peak is visible above the clouds and I can see the sea far below. I keep glancing back to see if it's still in sight, sad to leave it and promising to return one day soon.

Lessons Learned in Tenerife

- Pack using compression cubes. They really helped me to keep things organised in my suitcase and made the most of my space.

- Take a pair of travel scissors (with short, rounded blades for carry-on). These came in very handy for freeing my wrist from an 'all-inclusive' hotel band I had forced upon me.

- Use a money belt. I'd feel naked without mine now. It really gave me peace of mind having my passport, extra cash and a credit card safely tucked next to me.

- Think about how you want to spend time on your trip. I quickly realised I'd booked too many coach trips and had to reorganise things. Don't berate yourself for not seeing everything. Hopefully, there'll be another time.

- Don't take your bearings by the colour of buildings. I made a mental note to turn left by an orange building to find my way back to my hotel, but this obviously didn't work once it was dark!

- Remember that there is a stunningly beautiful, vibrant world out there – you just have to summon up the courage to leave your hotel room first!

Travel Day

It's two full months between my solo trip to Tenerife in February and my trip with G Adventures to Turkey in April. A strange in-between time which, if I'm going to travel more, is going to be a permanent fixture on the calendar so I guess I'll have to get used to it. But I'm feeling restless. I still have some of that nervous excitement from the first trip of the year to the Canaries, but there's also a cocktail of emotions about my next trip because this one is a bit different for me – the first trip where I'll be travelling solo but within a group.

When Saturday the thirteenth of April finally arrives, I'm more than ready for it. It's travel day and a chance to really test myself as it'll be the first time I'm travelling from Stansted airport on my own. I've downloaded the app for my flight and it isn't until I'm in the airport that I'm told there's a delay and, throughout the morning, it increases a little with each new update, resulting in a three-hour delay in total. The flight is only four hours so this almost doubles the travel time and doesn't endear me to Pegasus Airlines.

My former travel buddy, Rosie, gave me a very good tip for Stansted. Knowing I'm a fellow introvert, she told me how to find the quiet area and I wheel my suitcase towards the escalator to find it. My first impression is not good. The escalator is squeaking loudly and there are metal trolleys being unloaded so it's not particularly quiet, but there are definitely fewer people here and I choose a seat near a window.

It isn't long before a man and a woman – who appear to be work colleagues – land on a pair of chairs nearby and have a very loud two-hour conversation. I know it's this length because I leave and come back and they're still gossiping loudly and I don't believe the man is the type to ever sit quietly. The thing that baffles me is that they're both totally unaware of the unhappy glances from the quieter people around them and the frustrating thing is that nobody tells them that this is a quiet area – not even me. It does rather amaze me though that they don't realise that they're the only ones making a noise.

One of the places I escape to is the prayer room. I'm just so desperate for a genuinely quiet place to sit during my prolonged stay at Stansted. It's opposite the ladies' toilet so the constant blast from the hand dryers means that it isn't exactly peaceful, but it's certainly the stillest place I've found so far in the airport. I feel a bit of a fraud sitting here, but there's a young woman on the carpet doing what looks like school homework, and I'm sure I'm not the only one to have used this place as a haven.

The delay means that my plane now seems to be leaving at exactly the same time as the next plane to Istanbul – the flight I rejected because I didn't want to arrive after dark. This is very frustrating. Thankfully, the flight itself is uneventful, but it is most definitely dark as I exit the airport which makes me panic a little. This is my first time visiting the continent of Asia although I'm only passing through tonight as the transfer I've booked will be taking me to the European side of Istanbul across the Bosphorus into Europe. First, though, I have to find my transfer.

The first thing I notice about Istanbul is the smoke. Everybody, it seems, is smoking – the air is thick with it and my eyes instantly feel sore and gritty. I'm hoping that locating the transfer will be easy and I retrieve the notes I've printed out from G Adventures. I've located the pillar outside the airport exit and believe I'm in the right place but, after hanging around for a good ten minutes and making an unsuccessful phone call to the company, I ask a nearby taxi driver and he tells me to cross the road. I do this and hang around a little while longer before asking another driver who tells me to cross another road and to wait. It's warm and noisy and everything seems confusing. I'd so hoped to be at my hotel hours ago, maybe even with a little time to explore the city, but it'll be all I can do to fall into bed by the time I get there.

Finally, the man who told me to wait, approaches again and leads me to a vehicle and the journey from the airport begins. I'm aware that we're the best part of an hour away but the traffic at the end of Ramadan means a much longer journey and I arrive at my hotel at 11 p.m., having left home at 8 a.m.

It's been an exhausting day and it reminds me that I'm a long way off wanting to tackle a long-haul flight as yet. But I've made it. This morning, I was at home in a tiny Suffolk village. This evening, I'm in the heart of Istanbul. I've never been so excited in my life.

Travelling Solo Within a Group: Pros and Cons

Although this is my third solo trip, I'll be joining a group for most of my time in Turkey. I've arrived a day early and have booked a walking tour of the city through the tour operator as it seemed like the perfect way to get to know my way around and, to be absolutely honest, I'm not sure I'd have the courage to explore Istanbul on my own. My other two solo trips – to Crete and Tenerife – now seem positively tame by comparison and I wasn't at all daunted by Crete's capital, Heraklion. But Istanbul feels different. It's the most exotic place I've ever been and has a population of over fifteen million. I've tagged on three extra nights at the end of my tour and I'm hoping that today's tour of the city will give me the confidence and knowledge I'll need to go it alone later on.

I'm not sure if there's anybody else from my tour group here yet, but I look out for likely candidates as I go up to the sixth floor for breakfast. The room's flooded with sunlight and I gasp as I see the view – it's a fantastic panorama of the Golden Horn which leads into the Bosphorus Strait.

When I venture downstairs for the beginning of the tour, I see my name on a list with two others, Jill and Alex, and a little bubble of excitement rises in me. I'm not going to be on my own.

Our guide arrives and takes us three ladies via another hotel where we pick up some more people. They're here for the longer tour of Turkey which starts tomorrow as ours does. But where ours is eight days, theirs is fifteen. What's wonderful is that I've already 'met' somebody from this tour on a Facebook group and we say hello now. Her name is Anthea and I'm in awe of her recent trips to Morocco and Jordan. She's from New Zealand so, when she visits the northern hemisphere, she packs as much adventure into her time as possible.

And here's the thing with an organised tour – it makes you do things you might not have tried on your own. One of the first things we do is catch a bus to a part of town I probably wouldn't have thought to venture to. Here, we visit a castle and walk the backstreets where we see local pigeon sellers. The birds are huddled in boxes and seem very docile. They're also being handed around and we even see this happening in a car with a bird being passed from the back seat to the front. There are also cats everywhere – slinking along the pavements and sitting on doorsteps.

Our guide is young, enthusiastic and obviously cares passionately about Istanbul and knows his way around. He takes us to a tiny place for lunch which has been booked especially for our group of a dozen. And then we have our first free time in this huge city. Anthea, Jill, Alex and I walk off together. Anthea has her phone out, intent on finding the colourful houses she's seen online. At some point, and I'm not quite sure how it happens, Anthea and Jill disappear, leaving me and Alex to wander the streets alone together. We're mindful not to go too far from the meeting place and lose our way. And that's one of the first downsides I notice about being in a group. When you're on your own, it doesn't really matter if you wander off and get a bit lost. You've only yourself to worry about and you don't have the pressure of a timed tour. You can simply keep wandering – lost or not.

Once back with the group, we catch a tram to the river where we join a boat trip. It's busy and noisy and our group, wanting to be together, finds seats in the middle of the boat, under the canopy. It's not ideal. I'd been so looking forward to the boat trip and getting some good photos of the famous Istanbul skyline from the water so I sneak away from the group and squeeze myself into a seat at the edge of the boat. I'm aware that this might appear rude but I'm never going to get this opportunity again, I tell myself. Sometimes, you just have to do what's right for you.

While we're on the boat, I chat to our guide and I'm a little sad when he tells me that he'll be leading the longer tour and not our shorter one. It's amazing how quickly I've imprinted on him and now I feel a little discombobulated, and a tad anxious about meeting *our* guide later that evening.

But I needn't have worried for, when evening arrives and our group meets for the first time in the lobby of the hotel, our guide Ozgur is sweet and kind. We all cluster around on chairs and sofas and Ozgur asks us to introduce ourselves saying where we're from, if we've been on a G Adventures trip before and what we're most looking forward to on the tour. There's an older couple to my left and various other couples dotted around the room as well as women who appear to be on their own. It's a little like the first day at a new school when you're wondering who – if anyone – you're going to bond with.

It turns out that there are four other women travelling solo within the group: Jill and Alex who I've already met, and Sarah and Ella – so that's five in the group of fourteen. Alex, who's from Berlin, is the youngest. When I ask her why she travels solo, she tells me that she just got fed up of waiting for her friends' timetables, budgets and wish lists to align with her own. Ella from New York reveals how she was trying to arrange trips with her nieces, but they just didn't show any interest. She's also travelled with friends whose diets and eating habits have meant that she's the one to compromise which has affected her own well-being.

I'm so relieved that I'm not the only solo in the group. It takes the pressure off those awkward moments when everyone else is in a couple. Actually, when I do the maths, the solo female traveller contingency is the majority with five of us because there are only four couples plus Carla who is travelling with her son and daughter-in-law. It seems that the days of awkwardness for solo travellers might well be a thing of the past.

I like our group of fourteen – it's not overwhelming like the large group Roy and I once joined on a tour of Italy which filled a whole coach. Our little minibus-full is much more manageable – both in terms of navigating our way around places as well as navigating new friendships. I soon observe larger groups moving around ancient sites in a solid mass and I'm thankful that I'm not part of one of those as I'd find it much too tiring.

Our eight-day tour covers a lot of ground which means that we don't always get the time we want to explore somewhere. One such place is Ayvalik on the west coast of Turkey. We stop to eat at a place which Ozgur describes as a 'toast bazaar' and, when we enter, we're presented with around a dozen identical eateries to choose from, each with the same style of seating area in front. The speciality here is the toasted sandwich and they don't disappoint. The fillings are limited – they tend to revolve around cheese – but the speed, price and taste put a smile on everyone's face.

We're in Ayvalik to visit a small business championed by G Adventures. The shop supports local women and their products are made out of recycled goods. It's tucked away in town and we wend our way through the cobbled streets with quirky old buildings. Ozgur is on a mission and leads the way, but we're all getting hopelessly distracted. Ella wants to shop. There are colourful packets and tins of tea everywhere and she's clocked them all. And Jill and I obsess over the beautiful doors and windows, our cameras doing their best to capture the beauty, but we need much longer to do this place justice. However, our group timetable means we have to keep marching and that's one of the things you sign up to on a tour, I quickly realise. You must march at another's pace and, while that means you can fit a lot into a single day which you might not have been able to do otherwise, it also means you have to forgo a few sights along the way.

With a guided tour, you also hand over control when it comes to the accommodation, and choosing where to stay is one of the things I find most enjoyable about planning trips. I love looking for just the right hotel in just the right location. On the whole, the hotels on our Turkey trip are clean and comfortable with a good breakfast included. But there's one that stands out as quite bad. The usual one G Adventures books is being refurbished and this temporary one is certainly the kind of place you'd only stay in once.

My room smells of smoke and messages fly between us all on our WhatsApp group, checking to see if we're the only ones with issues. My shower head is broken and hangs limply and I have to hold it up to use it. And there's a terrifying hole in the wall with cables dangling out. I quickly decide that I will *not* be using the kettle. It's also noisy with car horns blaring in the streets, and the windy weather has all sorts of things clanging against the building which I don't want to think about. But at least we're only here for one night and I'm sure we'll all remember it with a wry smile – as long as we get out alive first.

Something else I find particularly hard while on the group tour is the routine of eating in the evenings. It's seen as a big part of the day when you can relax and socialise together. The trouble is, I just don't eat that late in the day or, if I do, I'm finished by six o'clock. Years of working from home and eating my main meal at lunchtime and then eating very lightly – if at all – in the evenings is a tough habit to break. I'm also absolutely exhausted by the time evening comes around and like to withdraw to my room to process the day and recharge for the next, but I'm horribly aware that this will seem antisocial. I get away with it a couple of times during the tour – on the very first night, I have quite a bad headache and retire early and, on another, I want to walk around town instead of going for a meal.

But I rally myself on the other evenings and it's lovely to spend this special time with the group especially on our final night together in Istanbul when Ozgur books us into a rooftop restaurant. There's also a delightful surprise as it's Amanda's birthday and her partner Andy has arranged for a candlelit cake to be brought to the table and we all sing 'Happy Birthday'. In that moment, surrounded by new friends in celebration and song in an exotic new city, I'm pretty glad I didn't retreat to my hotel room for the evening.

Helping, Caring, Sharing

What I find particularly lovely about touring as part of a small group is that we become a family unit very quickly and look out for each other. At the beginning of the tour, Ozgur sets up a WhatsApp group and we use this not only to share photos but to remind each other what time to meet for dinner or how to find the breakfast room in the hotel. But there are so many little instances of kindness during our week together that really touch me.

One lunchtime, Ella lends her glasses to someone, making us laugh as she casually hands them across the table so that one of our party can read the menu. On a visit to the hilltop village of Şirince, Kevin moves a concrete block to the side of the road after Carla trips over it. In the busy town of Selçuk, we walk together across the roads, making sure we're all safely across, and I play my part by giving Jill some ibuprofen and some suncream to Ella.

But the loveliest gesture of the week comes from Ozgur when we're in the minibus travelling between sites one day. Suddenly, we pull up by a stall at the side of the road and Ozgur leaps out, but I can't see what's going on. A moment later, he opens the door into the back of the minibus. He's carrying a huge crate of strawberries which he passes around before placing it on the table at the front. He tells us that his mother has made it through a difficult operation and it's traditional in Turkey to share your gratitude at such times with others. It's a delightful gesture that touches us all.

Moments of connection like this are the things we'll carry in our hearts long after we've forgotten the names of the archaeological sites we've visited. But there are some connections that go deeper than others and I find myself bonding with one particular person in the group: Carla. She's travelling with her son, Ken, and his wife, Nivi who, I think, are just a little bit older than me. I think it's wonderful that the three of them are happily sharing a holiday together. Carla tells me that a lot of people don't expect her to join in with activities at her age, but she tells me with a little smile, 'Be careful if you invite me to do something because I *will* say yes!'

What is it about certain people that makes you connect with them immediately? Carla and I go pretty deep pretty quickly – diving to the heart of life and discussing things that really matter. It just seems so easy. At one point, she says to me, 'Thank you for talking to me like I'm a real person.' I'm astonished by this and can't think how anybody else might have spoken to her in the past, but it seems as if her age might have affected the way people perceive her and that's a great shame.

I tell her about the recent loss of both my parents. I didn't plan to because I wanted my travel to be about living in the moment and really experiencing it. I didn't want to be stuck in the sadness of the recent past or dwelling on the difficulties of the not-so-recent past. But it's just so easy to talk to Carla.

'The only way through is through,' she tells me.

I've heard this before, but I stupidly keep thinking that I *am* through all the grieving even though it's not even been a full year since my mother died. The grief, I'm afraid, has its own timetable and the logical mind has no business being in charge. And it's as I'm talking to Carla that the grief creeps up on me again, ambushing me at the restaurant table where I'm stuck in the corner and have to push past everyone, excusing myself as quickly and as calmly as I can as I dash to the loos at the back of the restaurant.

Carla follows me, calling through the closed door.

'I didn't mean to upset you,' she says.

'You didn't. I'm okay,' I call back, trying desperately to stifle the sobs which seem quite determined to continue.

When I come out, Alex is there too. She saw me leave the table and was anxious. I feel so touched to have these two wonderful women caring about me and, when Carla hugs me, it really means the world. She's so much smaller than me, but her hug is so much larger. I never expected to make such a wonderful friendship so quickly.

Carla never told me her age and I didn't ask although I did surreptitiously ask her son later who told me she was eighty-four. But something Carla revealed was that, when people ask her age, they usually follow her answer with the word, 'Bless', which makes her want to throw them across the room.

During the week, Carla and I have rooms next door to each other on the second floor. When it's time to meet the rest of the group in the lobby to go out to dinner, I find it impossible to lock my door so I knock on Carla's.

'Can you lock your door?' I ask.

She admits that she's been struggling. We both try and try again, failing miserably at what should surely be a simple enough thing to do.

'I'll pop downstairs and ask for help,' I tell her.

Luckily, Kevin is sitting in reception so I ask him how he did it. Apparently, we should have pressed the button on the round door handle from inside. I frown. How do people like Kevin know to do something like this and people like me and Carla don't?

I run back upstairs and, laughing at our ineptitude, Carla and I finally manage to lock our doors.

It's while we're in Selçuk that we have the opportunity to book a traditional Turkish hammam and massage. Only half of our group opts to do this and, funnily enough, it's all women: Alex, Ella, Nivi, Dani and me and Carla. Carla and I choose to forgo the actual hammam. Instead, we book a one-hour massage and we're in adjoining rooms. Earlier in the day, Carla had a fall, giving us all a fright. However, she practically bounced up, much to everyone's relief, but I worry that she might be bruised from it and is now about to be pummelled. I have a woman masseuse, but Carla has a man.

However, just like her fall, she seems totally unfazed by the situation. I have nothing but admiration for her.

Carla is about half a minute ahead of me and, when I hear the happy slapping of flesh through the thin walls, I know what's coming my way. There is the occasional squelch from next door and I try desperately not to laugh. I'm getting pretty squelchy too.

After the massage, we meet Ella in the central space where we came in and we all have our faces painted with a grey mud which dries quickly in the heat, and we're given tea in tulip glasses. We then wash the mud off our faces and get dressed, and Carla and I wait for the others out in the sunshine. It's such a lovely moment to just sit with a new friend in a new country after a new experience. We're surrounded by vivid pink bougainvillea and spy a stork in its nest on the top of a nearby column. I tell Carla about Eckhart Tolle and the importance of truly being in the 'now'.

'I'll look him up,' she says.

'I think you'll get a lot out of his teachings,' I tell her.

We talk about how we both love to learn and evolve and I smile when Carla declares, 'I'm not the same person that I was last week.'

And there's an ache in my heart because I know that, after this week, I'll probably never see Carla again or even be able to keep in touch easily because she isn't on social media or email. But I try not to dwell on it because, as Eckhart Tolle tells us, life is *now* and, right now, I'm here with Carla having the very best time.

***

There's somebody else in the group that I find myself bonding with – Amanda. She's in her thirties and is travelling with her partner Andy. The two of them actually met on a G Adventures trip to Costa Rica. When Amanda finds out I'm a writer who lives in a thatched cottage with hens in the garden, she says I sound like a heroine from a romantic comedy which makes me laugh. I'd never quite thought of it like that before.

Amanda and I both gravitate to any stray animals that cross our paths and there are a lot of them in Turkey. When we arrive at the ancient city of Pergamon, we almost don't make it into the lift up to the site because there's a puppy by the entrance. He's trying to eat from a saucer of food and the stray cats that surround it are batting him away. We're both instantly smitten and, when we take the lift back down to find he's still there at closing time, Amanda doesn't want to leave him. How do the staff go home leaving him here to fend for himself? I don't think I could do it. Yet, I remind myself that this young animal – cute and small as he is at the moment – is going to grow into a huge dog soon. He has the same build and colouring as countless strays I've seen on the streets. It would be a full-time job to take them all in. But such logic is hopeless when you're face to face with a fluffy puppy.

There are more puppies when we arrive at the ancient site of Hierapolis. Amanda and I have to be corralled inside and back to the coach at the end of the visit. There are nine puppies – mostly golden – and they are playing under a sprinkler system, their coats gleaming with the water droplets. It's an absolutely irresistible sight for any dog lover.

***

But it's at Ephesus that I become aware of something else Amanda and I have in common. It's a windy day and the air is filled with dust. I put my sunglasses on and lower my hat for protection. I've noticed that Amanda is hanging back from the group. Andy is with her and somebody says that she's having a tough day with her migraines. My heart immediately swells in sympathy and I reach into my bag for the '4head' stick I carry with me. It doesn't banish pain, but it sometimes soothes it a little, making the skin tingle. When I approach Amanda with it, she tells me she has something similar. Her migraines are chronic, affecting her for twenty days or more each month. I can't even begin to imagine how that must feel. I know that I've let my three or four bad ones a year stop me from travelling in the past and Amanda acknowledges that she has done that too.

'But I'd spend all my time in bed,' she says, 'and I must live my life.'

She's sought specialist care and has medication, but it wears off long before the pain is vanquished.

Later in the trip, we talk about migraines some more – possible triggers and things that help. I ask Amanda what precautions she takes and she points out her sunglasses. I've noticed she wears a pink-tinted pair too which she says are good at night. She also has a wraparound pair but bemoans that they're not exactly flattering. She has a big bag of medications with her at all times.

We agree that, when we're in the grip of a bad migraine, it feels as if there's something trapped inside us that wants to get out and that the only release is often through tears, retching or screaming.

I feel such admiration for her as she joins in all the group activities. I sincerely do not know how she got herself around the enormous site of Ephesus that day with its dust-filled streets and crowds as I know how horribly painful and utterly depleting a migraine can be. But her spirit and determination to get on with her life and not miss a thing have inspired me so much.

Meeting the Locals

As this is my first trip travelling solo within a group, I'm noticing all the differences between this and the trips I've taken completely alone. For one thing, there is an understanding that you will remain with the group and this is put into practice each evening when it's assumed that everyone will dine together at the place the guide recommends. It's wonderful to have this option but one evening, when we arrive at the coastal town of Çanakkale, I decide to break free.

Ozgur gives us an orientation walk from the hotel down to the seafront and we all take photos of the huge model horse that was used in the movie *Troy*. It's an impressive sight but the real sight – for me at least – is the beautiful walkway along the seafront. The evening is warm and sunny and the last thing I want to do is sit indoors in a restaurant so, when Ozgur asks if we're all happy to go to dinner, I tentatively excuse myself and say I'd like to explore the town. It's been a tiring day and I need to be on my own for a while – finding that separateness that I relish on my solo trips.

I watch as the others walk away in the opposite direction from the one I'm taking and I can't help wondering if I've made a terrible mistake. I'm alone in a foreign town and I've just split from my group. What if I can't find my way back to the hotel? What if something happens to me while I'm on my own? I do my best to put my fears aside as I stroll along the seafront, admiring the stalls and restaurants before exploring the centre of town. I buy an orange juice from a little bar, watching as the man cuts open and squeezes at least four oranges into a cup for me. It's delicious and I explore the backstreets, smiling at the cats that seem to be enjoying their evening strolls just as much as the people.

When it's time to head back to the hotel, I'm pretty sure I'm going in the right direction. But here's the thing – I was only paying half the attention I should have been walking into town because I was talking to somebody in the group. Had I been on my own, I would have been paying a lot more attention. So I don't recognise the big shopfronts I'm passing and I want to be absolutely certain I'm going in the right direction before I go any further. Luckily, I took one of the hotel's cards on arrival and pop into a kiosk and smile, saying the name of the hotel and presenting the card to a young man. He doesn't speak any English and can't help me.

I walk back out onto the street and ask a man outside a shop, but he can't help either. It's then a woman approaches me. She's middle-aged and short with dark hair tied up in a bun. She takes the card I'm holding and motions to a street to our left. I follow her and she opens her handbag as she walks. I dare to look inside and see a plastic bag with what looks like cat kibbles. I smile as she motions for me to follow her and, a moment later, she points to a street to the right. There's my hotel, but she doesn't want me to go there. She points to the cat food and beckons me to follow her.

She stops at an entrance to an apartment block and unlocks the door. I have a moment's hesitation, but I can clearly see that this street is behind my hotel so I'm not too far away. I follow her inside and then the climb begins. We go up one floor, two floors, three floors… I begin to lose count. She stops when we're at the very top of the building in a communal area that is full of what appears to be junk. There by the banisters is a cardboard box and she motions excitedly towards it holding her phone up and telling me to do the same with mine. I approach the box and quickly see a female cat inside and what appears to be one tiny kitten. We both make encouraging noises and I watch as the woman decants the food from her bag and places it by the cat. She encourages me to take photos. It's an extraordinary moment. What was it about me that she connected with? Could she see my love for animals in my eyes? I show her some photos of the cats I've just seen in town that evening.

I've always counted myself lucky that I've never been abducted by a ne'er-do-well because I was the stereotypical little girl who would most likely have leapt into a stranger's car if they'd told me they had puppies I could cuddle. Indeed, even in my early twenties, I fell for that very line. I was working as a courier for SAGA Holidays in Cumbria one summer when I was an undergraduate. I only had one day off a week and loved to explore the local stately homes and gardens. One I remember particularly well. I got there quite late in the day and was completely enveloped by the romance of the lush, overgrown garden. It really was something out of a fairytale. As was the gardener. He was around my age and tall, dark and handsome. When he told me it was closing time but that I was welcome to stay, I was more than a little smitten. And then came the potentially killer line – he had puppies back at his estate cottage. Would I like to see them?

Reader, I went with him. Nothing sinister happened. I reasoned that he was an employee of a stately home, living in one of their properties and so he must be safe. It was probably a little naïve, but I lived to tell the tale and the puppies were very cute – as was the estate cottage.

So, here I am in Çanakkale, Turkey in my fifties – still falling for the 'puppies and kittens' line from strangers.

After a few minutes watching the kitten and its mother, I make to leave but the woman stops me and I watch as she goes downstairs and opens a door on the next floor, waving to me to join her in her flat. This isn't a good idea, is it? There's a part of me that really wants to follow her inside. Indeed, I've been reading a book about travel which encourages people to meet the locals because, so often on our travels, we only ever meet those in service: the hotel receptionists, the taxi drivers, the baristas etc. It's rare to really connect with local people. Well, here is my chance so I follow.

I don't feel comfortable removing my trainers as is Turkish custom, but I'm painfully aware that keeping them on might appear rude. Still, I wouldn't want to be without footwear if I suddenly have to make a run for it. I sit on the sofa which faces the door so that I have a clear exit ahead of me and I'm hugely embarrassed when my host places tissues under my shoes. I wish I could completely relax, but I know my husband would reprimand me for being here, and yet I know that my digital nomad friend would applaud me. Quickly, I WhatsApp Roy my location with the message: *I'll explain later!*

I use Google Translate on the phone to say a few phrases to my host and watch as she goes into the kitchen. It's an open plan living space so I watch as she moves around. I try to relax – I really do, but I can't help wondering if she's locked us both in or if there's anyone else in the apartment. She definitely wedged the main door open when we entered the block, I remember that.

After a few moments, she approaches me carrying a huge plastic bottle of what looks like blackcurrant cordial. I later find out that it is black mulberry juice – *karadut* – which is very popular in Turkey. She points to the bottle and taps her head. I think she's trying to tell me that it's good for the brain or memory perhaps. She pours some of the juice into two white cups on saucers. The juice is delicious. It's dark and very sweet.

She then brings out her wallet and shows me photos of a man who I assume to be her son. He is very handsome. And then something occurs to me for the first time. I have been sitting here having all these paranoid thoughts about her abducting me, poisoning me or robbing me. I've tried not to think of Stephen King's *Misery* where a writer is taken hostage – but she has made herself vulnerable too, hasn't she? She doesn't know who I am and yet she's invited me into the comfort of her home and has her wallet open in front of me, sharing intimate scenes from her life. It's a humbling moment. We are two strangers who met by chance, bonding over the cat and its kitten, sharing a drink, showing each other our photos and trying to communicate without language.

Once she really gets warmed up, she brings out some framed photos of her son on his wedding day and his beautiful bride. I feel very honoured that she's showing me some of the proudest moments of her life.

The funniest moment comes when she picks up her phone and calls somebody, holding it out to me to say hello. I feel like a celebrity as I talk to someone who I assume is a friend or relative. It seems that she's obviously excited by having an Englishwoman in her home.

I'm aware that it's beginning to get dark and I really should get back to the hotel. I use Google Translate to say that I'm meeting the tour party there. She shakes her head and points to the floor and then turns her hands into a pillow and places her head on them. She wants me to stay the night with her, doesn't she? I shake my head and reiterate that I must return to my group, my fear kicking in again in case she tries to make me stay. But it's okay. She simply rings her friend again for me to say goodbye. And then we hug and it seems like the most natural thing to do in the world. She takes a few photos of me as I leave the flat, asking me to remove my hat. I stand there on the landing of this apartment block, grinning like an idiot, feeling awkward but strangely cherished too.

As I walk back to my hotel, I can't stop smiling. I've met the cat lady of Çanakkale. I wish with all my heart that I'd been more relaxed, but I guess there's always that element of anxiety when you're on your own. One thing I know for sure, though, is that the encounter certainly wouldn't have happened if I'd been with our tour group. Indeed, I doubt it would even have happened if I'd been with my husband or a friend. Being on your own makes it easier for people to approach you. Of course, this isn't always good or safe or wanted, but it does open communication and makes for remarkable experiences.

The other chance I get to meet a local is in the bar of my hotel in Istanbul. I hadn't intended going there but, on my last solo day, when I simply cannot take any more of the noise and crowds of the city, I find myself back at my hotel by five in the afternoon. I had hoped it would be at least eight before I was back, but I'm absolutely exhausted. I've got a delicious fresh fruit cocktail bought at a street stall and I plan on having a little picnic in my room. Unfortunately, the neighbours are in and their toddler is kicking off. It sounds like the soundtrack from a horror film. I wonder if I'm fated never to find a quiet space of my own in this city, and then I remember that there's a small sitting area in the bar downstairs so I quickly leave my room, my fruit cocktail in my hand.

There's a man behind the bar when I enter and I just assume he's a member of staff until he sits down at the next table, a tulip glass of tea in his hand. We swap hellos and fall into an easy sort of chat. His name is Mehmet. He's around my age, wears glasses and is in Istanbul for work. He, too, has escaped noisy neighbours. We exchange smiles at that. We seem to have the same peace-seeking temperaments.

I tell him how noisy and smoky I've found Istanbul.

'Does everybody smoke here?' I ask him, genuinely thinking that they do.

He points to a sign in the bar which warns of a fine if people smoke and he tells me about a sultan who banned smoking.

'I think he might be my favourite sultan,' I say. I then tell him a bit about my time in the Grand Bazaar. Mehmet shakes his head. He disapproves of the pushy salesmen who intimidate tourists, but I tell him it was all good fun. An experience.

We talk about Brexit and quickly realise that we have something in common: we're two people who are desperate for our countries to belong to the European Union. Mehmet goes through the reasons he thinks Turkey has been refused entry in recent years and I tell him of some of the hatred that emerged in the UK during the Brexit campaign.

He asks about our royal family. What's happening with William and Harry? Do we want a royal family? It's an interesting and amusing discussion and fascinating to get an outsider's viewpoint on my country.

We talk about travel and how some places are so hyped up that they can end up disappointing tourists sometimes. He remembers his wife telling him about her visit to The Louvre in Paris where she saw the Mona Lisa.

'It's so small,' she bemoaned.

We also talk about language. Mehmet and his wife were recently chatting on a train when somebody asked what language they were speaking. When he said Turkish, they were surprised and explained how they knew lots of Turkish people, but their language sounded different. Mehmet explained how he spoke 'old' Turkish. Young Turkish people living in other European countries blend accents of the country they're living in with their own and so their Turkish becomes quite different. I tell him about the little Turkish school I used to teach at in London and how I was calling one of my students Cemal – I was pronouncing it 'See-mal'. One day, after weeks of me calling him this, my student patiently said, 'Miss, it's *Germal.*'

Mehmet laughs and glances at the TV which is showing a match on silent. He's a big football fan and used to play a lot until a knee injury. But he doesn't class himself as sporty and he talks a bit about sporty people.

'I'm not that kind of people,' he says, making me laugh.

It amazes me when I realise we've been chatting for two hours. It's like that with some people, isn't it?

The Last Day Together

It's a very exciting day for me: my first domestic flight. It'll only take an hour to fly from Denizli Cardak airport to Istanbul on the final full day of our tour but, as we arrive, we're not entirely sure that we'll be flying at all. The sky is stormy and there is thunder and lightning creeping ever closer. Ozgur has tentatively made arrangements in case we need to get back into the minibus and drive – an idea which doesn't appeal as it would mean spending all day on the road and no time for our tour of Istanbul in the afternoon.

Once we're through passport control, Ozgur and two others from our group walk across to the windows, looking out to where the plane waits. I join them. It's like a scene from a horror movie where the characters are trapped, wondering if they'll ever escape and fearful of what exactly is out there.

I return to my seat and Jill and I play a game, thinking of those in our group and how we would all be cast if this were, indeed, a film. I think Kevin is our hero – young and strong. Nivi would be the nurse – the maternal figure – kind and caring. David is a good, logical thinker. Ozgur is a natural leader, of course. I'd probably be the one to spot a stray dog on the concourse and risk opening the doors to let it in, causing possible chaos later on.

'We need a "final girl",' I say to Jill, explaining this key role. The final girl is the last one standing at the end of the horror film. She's usually the one to have spotted all the danger signals ahead of time. But who will our final girl be?

'Dani,' Jill says.

'Yes!' I agree. Young, smart and witty – if anyone could survive, it would be Dani.

Luckily, after only a short delay, we're able to board the plane. Our group has been split up, but I'm sitting next to Ken towards the back and we chat. He's very easy to talk to and he seems surprised when I talk about being an introvert. I explain to him that – although it's easy to talk one-on-one – as we are doing now, you'll rarely find an introvert so at ease in a large group. I tell him about my energy levels too and how, at the end of each day, I'm totally wiped out.

After a very bumpy flight, the landing is equally dramatic and we all give a round of applause once we're safely down. It might have been one of the shortest flights I've ever been on, but it's also one of the most memorable – as is the minibus ride into Istanbul back to the hotel where we started our trip. It's raining heavily and the traffic is at a standstill. We have a chance to be dropped off part of the way into town if we're willing to walk carrying our luggage, but none of us fancies it in the rain and, as we finally make a little progress through the traffic, the rain becomes even heavier.

'You wanted us to walk! We would be cursing you now!' Ella tells Ozgur and we all laugh.

A few minutes more pass and then we're all told to hop out as this is as close as we can get to the hotel today. Our driver has stopped and is out of the bus and we begin to disembark. But then a thud is heard as the bus lurches forward. What's happened? I'm stuck on the back seat and can't see.

'We've crashed,' someone says.

Once out, I see that our minibus has rolled into a yellow taxi. As our driver returns and reverses the bus, we see the dented side of the taxi. It's not good.

'He didn't put the handbrake on,' someone says.

'I saw what was happening, but it was too late.' Ozgur says.

It's been a rather eventful day's travel, but we make it safely to our hotel and, after a little rest, we meet in the lobby for our last tour with Ozgur. He shows us a few of the highlights of Istanbul – Hagia Sophia, the Hippodrome, the Blue Mosque and the Grand Bazaar.

That evening, we have our last dinner together and Ella calls for one last group photo to be taken outside the hotel. And then there's a strange, bittersweet moment as we all hang around the lobby. This is the final time we'll all be together and none of us seems to want to say goodbye. Dani and Kevin will be the first to leave for their flight back to Chicago in the early hours. And I'll be the last, staying on another three nights. I'll truly be the 'final girl', I realise. It feels a little daunting. How will I cope without my new pals? Will I be able to find my stride easily or have I now become reliant on having a guide and travel companions?

I remember a lovely quote from Charles Dickens's *Great Expectations*: 'Life is made of ever so many partings welded together.' We have truly become a little family during the last eight days and we all want to keep in touch, each of us inviting everyone else to reach out if we happen to be in their corner of the world. And, now that I'm more confident about my travelling abilities, I truly hope I get the chance to do that in the not-too-distant future.

The Time Alone

After spending eight wonderful days within the safety of the tour group, I now have three full days on my own. I'm in the largest, noisiest, most exotic city I've ever been to. On my own. At least I have the familiarity of the hotel as my home base. It's pretty central so it's easy to come back to during the day if I need to take a break, and the reception staff are friendly and I feel like a couple of them are keeping an eye on me.

What's most amusing on my first day alone is that I see David and Gail from our tour group – they've changed hotels, but are still in the same area so we have a little chat before saying goodbye.

And then I'm truly on my own.

There's that strange swirl of excitement and nerves again that I'm learning to recognise. As I'm planning to walk everywhere and not catch public transport, that takes a lot of the anxiety away for me. I can simply wander at a pace that suits me and, because I'm on my own, I only have myself to please. That's a very liberating feeling – to have a whole day opening out in front of you and to be able to fill it however you choose.

So I walk into the main square where the two great mosques stand. Ozgur gave us a brilliant tip to navigate our way back to our hotel – just follow the tram line. Well, as long as you remember which turn-off the hotel is on, I remind myself, making a note of the shops to look out for.

I am heading for the main attraction first: Hagia Sophia – the famous mosque dating back to the Byzantine Empire. I've heard the queue can be something else and it's pretty sizeable when I arrive. I have no idea how long it will take to reach the front. As I stand in line, I spot a guy touting for business as a tour guide.

'Sixty dollars,' he says. 'The cost of the ticket is thirty-five and you'll have a forty-five-minute wait. Come with me now and we'll be inside straightaway.' It's a convincing argument and I watch as two American women leave the queue with him, but can't help but smile when I reach the ticket counter in less than fifteen minutes and discover that the ticket is ten euros cheaper than the tour guide claimed.

Hagia Sophia is stunning. Since being converted from a museum back into a mosque, you can no longer walk across the ground floor, but the views from the gallery floor are wonderful. I have come prepared with a long blue scarf which I'm wearing over my head, but it keeps slipping as I gaze endlessly up into the gleaming gold domes above me. There are arches painted with fabulously intricate patterns and gold mosaics of saints showing the fascinating blend of religions inside this sacred building.

When I come out, I'm pretty peckish and spot the numerous carts selling street food. Usually, I find street food unappealing as it is often meat-based, but I'm delighted to see corn on the cob, roasted chestnuts and *simit* – a bread ring covered in sesame seeds for the equivalent of thirty pence. I buy a bag of chestnuts and find a bench to sit where I can enjoy them.

As this is my first full day on my own and I'm feeling pretty fresh and ready to take things on, I make the most of this to explore the area across the Galata Bridge. When I looked this up at home, it seemed like a pretty long walk and it was hard to gauge how long it would take, but I have the rest of the day so I set off.

The road is busy and the traffic is noisy, but the views across the water towards the Galata Tower and back to the famous mosque-dotted skyline of Istanbul are breathtaking. When I reach the tower itself, it's closed for restoration so I just wander the streets. It's Sunday and the area is heaving with locals and tourists alike. There are countless shops and restaurants and I'm looking forward to finding somewhere to eat here. But first, I walk.

It's always fun to wander – to go just a little further than the main tourist areas and to find where the locals live and I'm soon rewarded by some beautiful architecture and a glimpse into daily life in this part of town. I find a tiny church down some steps and what appears to be a chicken oasis – a little area of exotic trees underneath which hens are roaming. Actually one white hen has escaped and is on the street pecking at something tasty in a carrier bag.

I've just turned a corner when a man holding a phone out in front of him asks me for directions. You'll be lucky, I think. But he says the name of a church and I'm able to point him in the right direction as it's the very church I've just visited. It's so nice to be helpful to someone and to appear knowledgeable.

I take my time finding a place to eat and I'm delighted to spot the Frida House Café which is beautiful with exposed brickwork and colourful cushions. I quickly find a seat, but soon find myself enveloped in a cloud of smoke. There's a hookah smoker right behind me. He'll stop in a moment, I think optimistically, but he doesn't. After a few minutes, I have to admit defeat and move. And I'm so glad I do because this place is full of interest with shelves of books and beautiful lights and swing seats. I enjoy a huge bowl of salad before walking back across the Galata Bridge and heading into

the Spice Market. It's a lot less intimidating than the Grand Bazaar, which I'm still working up the courage to go back to without the group, but full of colour, scents and noise. It's hard not to succumb to the salesmen who offer free treats to entice you in for that big purchase. I take endless photos of the warm rich colours of the spices and the myriad teas with fun names like 'Love Tea', 'Viagra Tea' and 'Sultan Tea'.

I'm pretty tired by the time evening falls and need to change gears a little so head into Gulhane Park which isn't far from my hotel. It's full of couples and families and there are water features lit by coloured lights. The huge tulip beds are past their best now, but you can see how beautiful they were. I walk to the far end of the park and have a marvellous view of the Galata Tower across the Golden Horn.

When I leave the park as darkness falls, I can't resist seeing the mosques at night in Sultanahmet. They are lit up as are the fountains in the park between them. I walk and sit and stare, and I can't quite believe where I am and that I got myself here. It still seems extraordinary to me that I can venture from home and come to somewhere so far away and so very different. I stare in wonder at the Blue Mosque which looks almost pink at night, its slim minarets shooting up into the inky sky. And then I get up and follow the tramline back to my hotel.

It's been a packed first solo day and I work out that, when I'm away on trips, it's not unusual to do four, five or even more extraordinary things in one day. This would just never happen at home. If I have an event on when I'm at home – say a friend coming over or a day out, the next day is marked as a 'down day'. But you simply don't get the chance to do that during a short trip if you want to see everything. Still, as I return to the sanctuary of my room, I'm mindful of my energy levels and determine to take things a little easier tomorrow.

Panic at the Palace

The next morning, I make my way to the Topkapi Palace in the centre of Istanbul for opening time, figuring I'll beat the crowds. There's a queue, but I'm at the front of it in under ten minutes. I'm so excited to be here as it's one of the most beautiful places in Istanbul and was home to the Ottoman sultans for nearly four hundred years. Unfortunately, when I dive into the warren-like harem, I find that I'm one of many tourists in there who are trying to navigate the narrow passageways connecting the rooms. And there's soon a super snarl-up with French and Italian tour groups blocking the way as their respective guides give long descriptions of the rooms.

It's the longest hour of my life as I make my way through and, although there's so much beauty to look at, I'm finding it hot, crowded and way too noisy. As I queue for the treasury, I reach for my ear plugs which are soft and malleable in the warm weather. It is a blessing to mute the world if just a little.

I make my way around the jewels in the treasury. The famous Topkapi dagger studded with massive emeralds really is worth the wait in the long queue, but I'm glad to get back outside again. I then start to cough and find it hard to stop. Is it possible to contract a cold so quickly? Or worse – Covid? There were a fair few people coughing in the harem.

I am in total panic mode now because I can feel my tension rising. I'm in headache territory and need to calm down. There's still so much more I want to see here. I know I've only scratched the surface of this place, but I'm at my limit and need to get out. I quickly remind myself that the rest of Istanbul will be equally as crowded and noisy, so I have a long drink and sit down for a while before seeing a bit more of the palace.

My pledge to take things a little easier today has gone right out of the nearest Byzantine window. But that's easily fixed, I think, as I head back to my hotel for a couple of hours rest before starting out again later.

Feeling slightly less frazzled in the afternoon, I visit the Basilica Cistern whose Turkish name – Yerebatan Sarayı – means 'Sunken Palace'. Dating from early Roman times, it's an extraordinary

underground place made from more than three hundred recycled columns – some incredibly ornate and two featuring enormous Medusa heads. Created to store water to ease shortages during the summer months, it's a popular tourist destination today and it's used to showcase some beautiful sculpture.

A couple of days ago, I posted on the Facebook travel group, Solo in Style, saying I was in Istanbul, and Joanne from the UK reached out to me. After taking early retirement, she became a full-time traveller and is spending a few weeks in Istanbul. She has offered to

meet me this evening and, as I await her suggestion of where to go, I'm silently praying that it's somewhere easy to find – preferably somewhere I've already been to.

When her message comes through to meet at the Yeni Mosque, I panic, but I'm determined not to show myself up. I will work this out. It's pretty exciting to be arranging to meet someone in a foreign city. It feels rather intrepid and grown up; something a confident traveller would do. So I give myself plenty of time to find it and I'm delighted when I do as it's in a part of the city I might otherwise not have visited which is filled with lovely buildings housing interesting crafts. I have plenty of time so go into one of the shops and there's a young woman at the desk, surrounded by her art. Her manifesto is framed on the wall in Turkish and English and she's written that she's inspired by everything – even the whorls on her fingers can inspire art. I love this and we chat a little – her broken English and beautiful smile communicating her passion. And then it's time to meet Joanne.

I find my way to the front of the Yeni Mosque which faces the Golden Horn. It's a busy place with people queuing for the boats and there are stalls selling food. I buy a *simit* roll and find a spot to sit. As ever, I am early, but it's a good opportunity to soak in a bit of the local atmosphere. There are mothers with their children, commuters and stray cats – all jumbled together in the early evening sunshine. There are worshippers too and I watch as the men sit on small stone seats to wash their feet under outside taps before entering the mosque.

It occurs to me that the mosque is quite sizeable and I might actually be waiting at the wrong place, but it isn't long before Joanne shows up and we're on the move together. She's spent seven weeks living on the Asian side of Istanbul and is about to move on. We walk through the Spice Bazaar together and on to a very special mosque – Rustem Pasha. It's tiny compared to the better-known mosques and is decorated in exquisite blue Iznik tiles. We have it virtually to ourselves. It's just the kind of place Joanne loves to discover, she tells me and – with her spending longer in Istanbul than the average tourist – she has time to see so much more.

We have dinner together at a street café and, as darkness falls, we walk to Sultanahmet where, rather wonderfully, we run right into David and Gail from my G Adventures tour group again. In a city of millions, it seems extraordinary and wonderful that I can introduce everyone. The moment really makes me feel like quite the seasoned traveller.

When it's time to say goodbye to Joanne, I thank her so much for reaching out and for sharing a few of her special places with me. I silently thank myself too – for the courage to accept her invitation and for crossing a city on my own to meet her in a place I'd never been before. I'm quickly learning that there's a really supportive community of solo female travellers out there and, if you're confident enough to reach out to others, new friendships are just waiting to be made.

Of Mosques and Men

It's my last full day in Istanbul and I'm heading to the Blue Mosque. There's quite a queue and, as I wait, I prepare myself, covering my head with my scarf. It doesn't take long before I have my ticket and I'm soon on the steps, removing my trainers and placing them on a shelf to the right of the door. But, as I walk away, I realise that the exit is on the other side of the mosque and I'll be walking against a tide of people to retrieve my trainers, so I go back and place them on another shelf nearer the exit. Second shelf down on the far left. Nice and easy. I'll remember that. Should I take a photo? No, I'm being silly.

The mosque is busy. Built in the early seventeenth century, it's famous for its blue Iznik tiles and there are plenty of them, but the predominant colour to my eye as I gaze up into the spacious domes is pink. It's certainly one of the most beautiful mosques and I'm dazzled by the repeated patterns in the tiles and paintwork. How amazing it must have been to see this under construction. I wonder how many artisans were involved in its creation.

When I go to retrieve my trainers, I have a moment of blind panic when I can't find them. I pace up and down looking at the shelves, trying to spot them. There are so many black trainers and shoes, but I can't see mine. Has somebody taken them by mistake or even stolen them? I envisage walking through the streets of Istanbul in my insubstantial socks. I don't even have a spare pair of shoes at the hotel. I was determined to travel as lightly as possible on this trip. Well, I might be about to pay the price for that.

After a good few minutes of pacing up and down, I locate my trainers and it's with great relief that I slip them back on outside the mosque and continue with my day.

I'm looking for the entrance to the Grand Bazaar. How difficult can it be? After all, it's the world's biggest shopping mall. It shouldn't be hard to spot. I take a break from a rather lengthy walk and look around me. I'm in a large open square with a fine view of two mosques ahead of me. I take a few photos and, as I'm putting my phone away, a man pops out of nowhere to my right.

'Do you like the mosque?' he asks nodding towards the one straight ahead of us.

'Yes,' I say.

'Would you like to know its name?'

'I would,' I say cautiously. Is he a tour guide? I've heard it's incredibly hard to get shot of one if they latch onto you.

He tells me the name, but says the other, more distant mosque, is his favourite.

'I can take you there,' he says.

'No, thank you,' I tell him. 'I'm meeting friends at the bazaar.' It's a handy line to roll out even if it isn't true.

'Where are you from?' he asks, undeterred. And so it begins – a playful back and forth of questions – both of us pretending to be interested in one another. His name is Arif and he's very charming.

'My shop is just over there,' he says, motioning behind him. *Aha!* We've got to the crux of the matter at last. 'Come and see my rugs.' He begins to tell me how special they are using words like 'unique' and 'tribal'.

'Nobody will have a rug like this,' he insists.

'I've got to meet my friends.'

'Let me finish my sentence,' he says and I laugh at his cheek. Some people might interpret it as rude, but he just strikes me as a wonderfully gifted salesman and I'm rather enjoying his performance – as long as I'm able to get away from him at some point very soon. I've heard some horror stories about shopkeepers not letting tourists go until they've been pressured into buying something. In fact, a couple from our tour group was followed by a man into a mosque. They just couldn't get rid of him and he turned quite nasty, saying they'd led him on. Luckily, after just a little awkwardness, I'm able to walk away and find the entrance to the Grand Bazaar.

Almost immediately, I'm entranced by the shops and find myself inside one, looking at the silver and turquoise earrings. When the owner sees my interest, he goes to get more for me to choose from, leaving his shop. He's gone a fair while and I wonder at the trust he has placed in me. When he comes back with three pairs of earrings which really aren't my style, I express an interest in a tiny sparkly pendant – a representation of the 'evil eye' featuring tiny round turquoise stones. I've seen them all over the city and I've previously been tempted by a pair of earrings, but this tiny pendant is calling to me so I ask the price. When he says it, I purse my lips and have a go at haggling. He's willing to come down one hundred Turkish lira and

I nod happily. I have now haggled in the Grand Bazaar of Istanbul and have a lovely piece of jewellery to remind me of the moment.

One of the very next shops I see has bowls of crystals outside. I have a real weakness for crystals and can't resist looking. Of course, this gets the attention of the young shop owner who invites me in to see more.

'I'm only looking,' I tell him, thinking of the purchase I've just made and that I'm really not planning to buy anything else. He smiles and invites me in again. We introduce ourselves. His name is Ismail.

The shop is small and absolutely packed with gems. It's a dazzling sight and I enjoy looking at the enormous silver-set gemstone cuffs, the pendants and earrings, and the raw and polished crystals. I ask Ismail if he has a favourite stone and he tells me he likes everything. I can see why.

When he offers me tea, I become anxious that he might be about to launch into some hard selling, but I'm really not getting that vibe from him and I've read that tea is often offered to customers so I thank him. He calls to someone outside who appears a few moments later with apple tea in a tulip glass on a saucer and tray. It is sweet and delicious and I feel thoroughly spoilt.

He tells me that his family owns four shops and he's keen to show me another in Istanbul, but I really don't have time. It sounds like he works hard. He only takes Sundays off and never has a holiday. I'm shocked by this admission and tell him that he must! Now that I've discovered travelling, I'm quite evangelical about it. And, during the whole time I'm in his shop, he really doesn't try to sell me anything. He just seems happy to talk and his English is very good indeed.

I feel quite sad to leave Ismail, but I'm aware there is so much more to see in the Grand Bazaar and I'm excited to discover a row of lamp shops. There's a young Turkish man sitting outside one and he invites me in. His name is Belmut.

'Is it okay just to look?'

'Of course!' he tells me, ushering me inside.

I'd been hoping to see inside one. The lamps are so magical with the different patterns and colours and I'm mesmerised. There are warm oranges, vivid reds and pinks, lime greens and ocean blues, and dazzling silvers and golds.

Belmut points out some of the delightful filigree pieces towards the back. They're enormous – like large metal balloons.

'Pick one up,' he says. 'They're light. Try!'

I do and he's right. They're so wonderfully tactile that it's hard to put it down.

He asks me which I like most and, of course, I tell him. He then does his salesman bit.

'We can ship to anywhere. It's no problem.'

I have to smile. I walked right into that one.

I say goodbye to Belmut, deciding it's time to leave the Grand Bazaar. My eyes – *all* my senses – have absorbed enough and I think I've got away lightly with just one very small purchase. It's not until later that I realise I completely forgot to see the section selling carpets. But you can't see everything – at least, not in one day.

I walk through part of the city I've not yet explored. It's my final afternoon here and I'm beginning to flag. My eyes are sore with hay fever and the cigarette smoke that seems to be everywhere. And the noise is getting to me.

I visit a *turbe* – a mausoleum full of tombs – each covered with thick coloured fabric. The grounds are full of extraordinary tombs too – some with engraved columns on the top. I spot a gravestone featuring musical instruments and, with the help of Google, find out that it marks the resting place of a composer. Some of the graves are a little overgrown and I spot a cat sleeping in the deep grass.

I visit a few other sites before calling it a day. There is so much more I could see, I know, but I've reached my limit. It's been a truly wonderful trip, but my body is telling me it's over. I am happily saturated with all the places I've seen and the people I've met. Turkey has been such an adventure, and Istanbul has filled me with so much awe and inspiration. As I leave the noise of the city behind me and make my way back to my hotel, I can't help wondering if I'll return one day.

Moments

One of my favourite actors, James Stewart, once said that, when he read a script, he looked for 'moments'. As a writer, moments are something I'm very aware of too, but I'm becoming more aware of them in my own life now.

A single trip is made up of so many moments and it's always a joy to recollect them and to share them as stories. There are moments I would sooner forget, of course, like the pure panic I felt trying to find my transfer from Istanbul airport; losing my trainers at the Blue Mosque and becoming overwhelmed in the Topkapi Palace. But, luckily, there have been so many more moments of joy on this trip like sitting on the steps of the theatre at Hierapolis with Ella, Jill and Amanda – the four of us sharing a few moments of silent awe together; swimming above the Roman columns in the pools at Pamukkale with palm trees and swallows above me; one of the salesmen at the rug workshop picking up his saz and serenading us as we drank sweet tea in the sunshine; the cat lady of Çanakkale sharing her family photos with me, and Ozgur buying us all strawberries.

And perhaps all these memories mean that I am learning to live more fully in the present moment.

One morning as our group met in reception before leaving our hotel, Ken said to me, 'You always look so happy.'

'I'm just amazed to be here,' I confessed.

Well, I hope that feeling of joy and awe never diminishes and that the moment-filled adventures continue for many years to come.

Lessons Learned in Turkey

- If you're anxious about travelling solo, it's great fun to do it within the safety of a group. I was one of five women travelling solo on my G Adventures trip. A tour is always a fantastic way of covering a lot of ground without the hassle of organising it all yourself.

- If you decide to go anywhere on your own, let your group know – especially if you end up in a local's home!

- Be open to talking to locals, but be mindful that some of them will simply be trying to sell you something!

- Know your own limitations. I found the crowds, noise and smoke of Istanbul overwhelming. I don't regret my time there but one day fewer might have made all the difference to my energy levels.

Vienna Waits for You

I take a deep breath. In my head, I've been planning a very special trip for a while now, but it has only been *in my head*. The truth is, it's scaring me witless because I've never done anything quite like this before. It's a trip that will involve four cities, two planes, two train rides, a boat, countless metros and trams and eleven nights spent in four different places of accommodation. And travelling with a backpack which I've never used before. But it's time. I need to do this so, one morning in early March, I book two separate flights – one from Stansted to Vienna and one from Budapest to Stansted. It's the first time I'll ever fly into one city and fly home from another – and travel between the two of them by train. There are *countless* ways that this could all go wrong.

Once my flights are booked, I book my accommodation starting with two nights in a hostel in Vienna and three nights in a hotel. I haven't stayed in a hostel for over thirty years and I'm excited to see what they're like now, but anxious in case there aren't any older people there and I find it all a bit too noisy – hence the three nights in a hotel. After Vienna – which will include a day trip by boat to neighbouring Bratislava in Slovakia – I'll be taking the train to Salzburg where I've booked three nights in a small apartment. It's another first for me and I'm a little anxious about finding my way there, obtaining the key and hoping that everything in the apartment works and that I'm not floundering around with faulty light switches or anything. That's the joy of a hotel over private accommodation – there is always somebody at reception to ask for help. From Salzburg, I'll be taking a train to Budapest where I've booked three nights in a beautiful hotel with a rooftop pool. I'm really looking forward to that one. A lovely treat to round off my trip.

During the booking process, I nearly mess up and book one night too few in Salzburg, but I catch my error in time. It's more coordination for a trip than I've ever handled before which is both exciting and terrifying. This trip really feels different from anything I've ever done before. Turkey might have been my most exotic location to date but, although I had a few days solo in Istanbul, all I really had to do was find my way to the hotel and the rest was taken care of for me. But Austria is the big one. I just hope I won't let myself down.

***

I catch sight of my reflection at the airport. Who is this woman? I feel like a tortoise and, with the unusual weight of the backpack, I'm moving as slowly as one. But how liberating this feels. I have one of those *I could go anywhere from here* moments. I have everything I need strapped to my back.

Leaving Old Thatch this morning was so hard. The garden is surging into spring. It's peak wisteria time and the first rose, a pink and perfect Albertine, has opened in front of one of the kitchen windows. Of course, it was hard leaving Roy and my spaniel Hattie and our little flock of hens too. But it was time for me to go.

I have watched so many vlogs about the transport system in Vienna and, once I've landed and gone through passport control, I make my way to the train station – looking out for a ramp which leads down to the ticket machines.

Once I have my ticket, I see a smartly dressed gentleman waiting for the train and I ask him if I'm on the right platform for Wien Mitte. He tells me that I am and we board the train together a moment later and sit opposite one another and chat. His name is Christian and he's an Austrian pilot and he talks about the time he visited London believing he could walk easily to the Tower of London from Piccadilly. It makes me feel a little better knowing that someone as capable and intelligent as a pilot can still feel uncertain in a new city.

I ask Christian where a pilot goes on holiday and he tells me how much he loves Greece. I mention that I went to Crete and Santorini last year and he tells me that, when he flies over Santorini, he tilts the plane a little so that the passengers can see the white houses. But, as much as he loves Greece, he adores staying at home. I suppose when you travel as part of your job, home becomes very special indeed.

I tell Christian my plans to visit Bratislava from Vienna by boat and my excitement to see Salzburg. He confesses that he's never seen the film *The Sound of Music*. I had heard that Austrians weren't as in love with it as the rest of the world, but it does seem amazing to me seeing as the film is one of the main reasons I'm here in Austria.

The train arrives at Wien Mitte and I say goodbye to Christian, feeling happy to have made a connection with a local so early in my journey. I change to the metro and buy a one-week ticket. Again, I saw this advice on a vlog and it represents very good value. I'm hoping it will make my life easier because you can use it across all the buses, trams and metro. The other huge plus is that I only have to validate it the first time and, unlike London's underground, I don't need to keep swiping. I just have to make sure I have it with me at all times in case I'm stopped by an inspector as there's a hefty fine if you don't have a validated card on your person.

This is the first time I've not booked a transfer from the airport when travelling alone. But the directions I printed out from the hostel's website seemed so straightforward that I really wanted to give it a go on public transport.

I find my way to Kettenbrückengasse and leave the metro, surfacing near the Naschmarkt. The trouble is, there are no more directions to the hostel once you come out of the station and, unfortunately, there are all sorts of ways I could go wrong here because there are so many exits and different directions I could take.

There is still a little light in the sky, but I'm travel-weary now. I spot a couple of women chatting nearby and approach them. It's only after five minutes of walking the wrong way that I realise they've given me the wrong directions. I ask a couple outside a bar. It's getting dark now and I really need to find my accommodation. The couple sends me back the way I came and I discover that I was literally just across the road from the hostel when I first came out of the metro station.

When I finally make it into the reception area, there's an Irish singer performing and about a dozen people sitting round to watch. I'm immediately taken back to the evening entertainment in the hotel I was staying at in Tenerife, only, when this guy plays, it's a much nicer sound.

It feels funny checking into a hostel. The last time I did was when I was working for the civil service in Carlisle. I had only recently met Roy (incidentally at a youth hostel in the Peak District). He was living and working in London and used to drive up to see me in Cumbria whenever he could, and I would save up as many days as I could by working flexi-hours. We had very little money and would have long weekends away, camping or staying in hostels in Wales, Northumberland or the Yorkshire Dales.

Now, here I am, in my first hostel since my early twenties and I'm pleasantly surprised. I have a double en suite room to myself which is spacious and clean and surprisingly quiet. It's not as pretty as a hotel room, of course – there's no fridge or kettle or fancy paintings on the wall. It's a stripped down, functional space.

If I was really to push myself, I should have the briefest of rests and then go downstairs to listen to the evening entertainer and attempt to meet some of my fellow hostellers. But my travel day has taken absolutely everything I have to give and, as I unpack, I congratulate myself for making it here at all – from getting on a plane by myself to navigating my way from the airport on public transport while carting my backpack. I might just be turning into a real traveller at last.

The First Day

My first morning in Vienna is wet and cool and I reach for my red umbrella before leaving the hostel. There is a free guided tour of Vienna which leaves from the hostel and I'm keen to join that, but it doesn't leave until 10.30 a.m. which means I have time to pop out, buy some breakfast and find my first film location.

It's not just *The Sound of Music* that's brought me to Austria – it's another film too: *Before Sunrise* – a gorgeous 1995 romantic drama directed by Richard Linklater and starring Julie Delpy and Ethan Hawke who play Celine and Jesse – strangers who meet on a train and decide to get off to explore Vienna together, for one night only. When I was looking at the locations where they filmed, I discovered that one of my favourite scenes was shot in a street very close to my hostel so I head there now.

Finding film locations can take you on all sorts of little adventures and I feel like I'm on one of those as I explore the quiet backstreets of Vienna. I pass *The Third Man* museum – another iconic film shot in this city – and you can see why because even the backstreets are beautiful.

It might seem odd to some people that I'm looking for a pair of ground floor windows, but I'm so excited when I find them. They're in a residential area and still look just as they did in the film with their ornate green grates. Luckily, it's quiet here and there is nobody around as I feel a little self-conscious taking photos of a pair of windows, but it was here that Celine and Jesse took photos of each other – only they didn't have cameras. Instead, they just took a moment to gaze at one another. It is truly one of the most beautifully romantic scenes in film.

The streets are glossy with rain as I look for something to eat – something cheap, wholesome and portable. I don't mind eating on the move – it means I can see more things.

As I head back the way I came, I can see that some of the stores are open at the Naschmarkt and I quickly find one selling nuts which I'd hoped to find as they're an important part of my do-it-yourself breakfasts when travelling. The two men serving are from Cairo and one of them quickly engages me by giving me a couple of treats for free. Then it's on to the selling. I tell him I'd like a variety of nuts but, as they're all different prices, he starts decanting them into separate bags, using a large metal shovel.

'That's *way* too much!' I keep saying, but he's not listening and I'm swept up in his banter as he goes from nut to nut.

'No!' I protest. 'I'm travelling light – I have to carry all this on my back!' I'm beginning to feel a little helpless and, by the time he's finished, he's collected half a dozen bags. It's more than I'd ever buy or eat in a month let alone twelve-day trip. He hands them to his colleague and promptly disappears, and his colleague weighs them.

'Thirty-six euros,' he tells me.

I gasp. 'I can't afford that!' I say. 'I wanted small amounts.'

He shakes his head. 'I've put it all through the till now.'

I feel panicky. 'You're not listening to me. I can't pay for all those nuts.'

'Thirty euros,' he says. 'You pay just thirty.'

'No.' I remain adamant, but he keeps insisting I buy them. 'You're scaring me now,' I tell him and walk away.

He calls after me. 'What do you want?'

I stop and return. So, *now* he's listening to me.

'Two of those bags. Just two.'

He nods, gives me a price and I hand him the money. When I check, I see he's shortchanged me – obviously deliberately – but I don't challenge him. I need to get as far away as I can. The whole encounter has left me shaking and has rather spoilt my first morning in Vienna.

Fortunately, the walking tour from our hostel is a wonderful distraction. It's led by Katrina who's wearing a bright blue woollen suit and a yellow beret so there's no chance of losing her. She starts by pointing out some of the buildings I've photographed already that morning, and then she takes us into the market and I begin to panic as we walk on and on – coming dangerously close to the Cairo nut sellers. Luckily, we divert just before we reach them.

It's a wonderful tour and it really gives me the confidence to walk between sites, and I'm particularly keen to do that in the afternoon as I want to see the famous Klimt paintings at the Upper Belvedere and it seems tricky to get there by public transport. I make three attempts and I'm on the verge of giving up when I spot the nearest metro station and go in to buy a sandwich and ask the server which is the best way to go. She tells me to take the metro and then the train. Somebody else tells me to take the tram and walk. In complete confusion, I end up at St Stephen's Cathedral and decide to do the tour of the crypt while I'm there. But I still want to see the Klimt paintings so I make one more attempt. It's one of Vienna's top tourist sites so thousands of people are obviously managing to find their way there and I'm jolly well going to be one of them even if I have to walk right across the whole city.

Walking, however, has its benefits and allows me to notice the trams, and I see that tram number one goes to Prater amusement park which is perfect as that's where I'm hoping to head this evening. I'd originally planned to get the metro, only I'm not sure where the nearest station is and I don't want to spend any more time today walking in the wrong direction.

But the Klimt paintings are worth every minute it's taken to get here. Housed in a Baroque palace, the enormous windows look down onto a parterred garden with stunning views back towards the city. The white balustraded staircase and ornate ceiling make me feel as if I'm in the middle of a wedding cake, and I'm thrilled to find paintings by Monet and Van Gogh here too. But – oh – the Klimt's! I'm almost too nervous to see the most famous one, entering a couple of rooms anxiously, not knowing if it's in them. Of course, there's no missing it because there's quite a crowd around it and a seat has been placed opposite it, so you can sit down and absorb the fullness of its beauty. And how the gold gleams.

Austrian artist Gustav Klimt painted 'The Kiss' in 1907 during what became known as his 'Golden Period'. One of the most famous paintings in the world, his use of gold and mosaic-like detail is thought to have been influenced by Byzantine art. It's in a very simple black frame so as not to detract from its beauty and it's a little smaller than I'd imagined it would be. That thought makes me remember what Mehmet in Istanbul said about his wife being disappointed by how small the Mona Lisa was. We build these things up in our minds. Still, whether larger or smaller than we imagine, these paintings draw us to them and, when a space becomes available, I sit opposite 'The Kiss' so I can stare at it for a little longer. After all, it took me quite a few hours – and even more years – to find my way to it.

Once I've taken in as much beauty as is humanly possible, it's time for some fun so I catch a tram from the Upper Belvedere which will take me all the way to Prater. I feel very clever to have discovered this tram – quite accidentally – as I believe it has saved me a long walk to the nearest metro station. I ask the tram driver where I can catch the metro home and he tells me the station is on the other side of the park. I'll have to trust that I'll be able to find it later. I'm not quite prepared for the walk to the actual entrance of the amusement park, but it's pleasant in the early evening light. My way is shaded by trees and there are joggers and cyclists galore. I'm pretty sure I'm heading in the right direction. The world's oldest Ferris wheel would be pretty hard to miss, I imagine.

That's what I'm here to see: the famous Ferris wheel which featured in *The Third Man* – where Orson Welles gives his famous 'cuckoo clock' speech – and where the first kiss in *Before Sunrise* takes place. On my way to the wheel, I walk by many tempting rides, but I'm aware that it will be sunset soon and I want to be on my way back to the hostel before darkness falls as I still don't know the way to the metro.

The Wiener Riesenrad was constructed in 1897, but many of the thirty gondolas have been replaced since then and you can see a few of the originals in the museum under the Ferris wheel which you enter as part of your ticket.

The views from the top of the wheel across the park and city as the sun goes down are really breathtaking. I ask a fellow passenger if they'll take some pictures of me and I take some of them. I think of Celine and Jesse's romantic moment up here in the Viennese sky and I can't help wishing that Roy was with me. I know he'd love this.

Once I've come back down to earth, I have to find my way out of the park and I'm hoping that the metro station is a lot closer than the tram stop was. Luckily, after asking someone for directions, I'm at the station in less than five minutes.

When I get back to the hostel, I think about the amazing first day I've had in Vienna. Had I been with a partner or friend, I probably wouldn't have been taken advantage of by the market sellers, I might not have taken quite so long to find my way to the Upper Belverdere, and it would no doubt have been a lot of fun to share the joy of the Ferris wheel ride. But I handled, coped with and enjoyed everything on my own and that gives me such a thrill.

Crossing the City

I'm on the move today. As much as I've enjoyed my stay in the hostel, I wanted to experience a Viennese hotel too and I had time to do both with five nights in the city. So I pack up my backpack and check out. I've worked out the metro stations nearest the Theaterhotel. Alas, when I arrive at the metro, I discover that the three stops I'd earmarked as possible to walk from are not operating. I'm going to have to get the tram which is probably better as I will actually be able to see where I'm going and get a feel for distances. But the thought makes me nervous even though I took a tram the day before. Still, I have my ticket and need to do this otherwise it will mean a long, hot walk with my backpack.

The stop I want is near Parliament – a distinct white classical building which should be impossible to miss. But, when I get off the tram, I'm not sure which direction to go. It's sunny and bright and my backpack is comfortable, but I'd rather not be walking miles in the wrong direction with it. I know the name of the street and I'm pretty sure I'm there, but I can't see the street name so I dither about. I get my phone out to use Google Maps, but the sun is so bright and it means faffing about with my glasses, so I put it back and try the old-fashioned way by asking someone.

I spot a man in a bright blue jacket. He looks smart, official and approachable. It turns out that he works at the Columbian embassy and he kindly tells me I am, indeed, heading in the right direction so I continue. I silently reprimand myself; I have so little faith in myself sometimes. But I still can't see a road sign so I ask a lady walking her dog. She's obviously local and dog walkers tend to know their way around. She confirms that I'm to go straight ahead although she suggests a side road, but my instinct is telling me to keep to the main one where I believe the hotel is and, a few minutes later, I find it.

I thought I'd be way too early to check in, but hoped that they'd be able to take my backpack until I returned in the evening. However, I get lucky and I'm allowed to go straight to my room – a small suite with a little living space upstairs and bed and bathroom downstairs. It feels very luxurious after the hostel and I'm looking forward to a relaxing bath in the evening after all my walking. The danger here is that I might hide out in my suite for a little longer than I should after my slightly stressful journey across town.

I message Aussie Vicki – the traveller I met on a day trip to Santorini (see my book *Introvert Abroad*). I tell her about my morning, confessing that I had been heading in the right direction all along only I didn't have any confidence in myself. She messages me back:

'Start trusting yourself. You are doing this and doing it well! A bit of anxiety in a new place is to be expected. But, from your photos and what I hear in your words, you are having the time of your life. Super soloist!'

It really buoys me up to have such a wonderful cheerleader. But maybe I will always feel that nervous thrum of energy when I'm travelling. Still, I am determined to leave the hotel promptly and have a fabulous day.

I soon discover that there's a tram I can catch just down the road from my hotel that will take me around the Ringstrasse – the impressive circular road that passes many of Vienna's finest buildings. It's the perfect hop-on hop-off transport for the rest of my time here and I take one now to the centre of the city.

I walk to the Baroque church of Karlskirche, but the Rick Steves' guidebook I read is two years out of date and there is no longer a lift to take you up into the dome. However, you can walk up steps to the organ loft and to the roof for some fine views.

When I come back down to earth and sit on a pew, the midday light is streaming into the church. I'm in exactly the right place at the right time as I spot a priest walking down the aisle. I scoot along my pew and capture a photo of him.

It's warm and I'm tiring as I leave Karlskirche. I need to find something to eat quickly – a proper sit-down meal as I've just been snacking while walking so far on this trip which is a bad habit to fall into when you're on your own and aren't accountable to anybody. This, of course, can be an advantage as you can save both time and money, but it might also mean your diet isn't the best and you could easily find yourself running on empty.

I find a pretty café in a park surrounded by trees. There's a man sitting nearby who looks like a character from a Chekhov play – some kind of student or revolutionary. I watch as he lights a cigarette. Unlike the UK, smoking is still allowed here in public places like restaurants. I order a Greek salad, fries and a diet coke to ward off the beginnings of a headache. I really needed this sit-down

meal – to give myself a moment after the rush and excitement of the past two days.

In the afternoon, I take a guided tour of the opera house before getting on a tram to go back to my hotel for a rest. However, I don't make it back to my hotel on the first go because the tram loops around Parliament, taking me back the way I came. This totally knocks my confidence as I was so sure I'd sussed things on the tram front.

I get off and try again.

Thursday means it's late-night opening at the Kunsthistorisches museum and I take full advantage to get the most out of my time in Vienna. So, after resting and eating at my hotel, I head back into town and enter the museum. Opened in 1891, it took twenty years to build and its ornate interior is worth seeing even if you aren't interested in the fabulous collection within it.

I start in the sumptuous Egyptian rooms before finding my way to the Tudor portraits. But it's a stunning if rather gruesome painting of the Medusa's decapitated head which really captures my attention. You can almost see the snakes still writhing.

There are so many treasures in this place and I'm sad to leave. Out on the Ringstrasse, I catch my last tram for the day, delighted at having seen so many beautiful things and happy to have navigated my way around the city, meeting so many kind people along the way who made sure I was going in the right direction.

City of Horses

It's my final full day exploring Vienna. I walk from the hotel to the local shops. It's just after seven in the morning and everything is closed so I can't yet grab anything for breakfast. So I wander. And wonder. This is my favourite thing to do in a new place – simply walk the streets, taking it all in: the buildings, the people, the trees – everything. I love spotting and photographing quirky doorways and pretty windows. But, while I love to just drift, I'm mindful of the location of my hotel so I don't get completely lost. I have a timed ticket for a special event later this morning and don't want to be late.

I'm getting used to walking down the hill from my hotel to catch the tram into town. It's funny how quickly one adapts to a new routine. I can't help remembering that it was just yesterday that I was in panic mode as I tried to find my way around this area.

I get off the tram at the opera house. I have a ticket for the Spanish Riding School and find my way to the area where I believe it to be. It's part of the enormous Hofburg complex and I see the stable courtyard. There's a digger removing some of the soiled bedding and the white head of a horse pops out of one of the stables. I'm definitely in the right place.

After finding the ticket office and swapping my paper printout for a proper ticket, I ask where I go next. This isn't the building, I'm told. I have to go back outside the way I've come. I panic. What if I can't find it? There are so many arches and doorways in this place. But I needn't have worried because I soon spot an absolutely enormous queue of people waiting for the show.

I've booked a standing ticket to see the morning training session with the famous white Lipizzaner horses and, when we enter the arena, I gasp at its beauty. As part of the Hofburg palace, it has an ornate plaster ceiling, elegant columns and giant chandeliers. When the music begins and the horses appear with their uniformed riders and handlers, it really is a sight to behold. It strikes me that, where Istanbul smelled of cigarette smoke, the city of Vienna smells of horse. They are almost everywhere you look – from the famous Lipizzaners here to the ones giving carriage rides around the city. Vienna loves its horses.

I remain within the Hofburg complex for the rest of the morning, visiting the Butterfly House – or *Schmetterlinghaus* – mesmerised by the dazzling blue beauties who dance in the warm air above the exotic plants in the glasshouse.

After a sandwich on a park bench, I do my best to find the Ephesus Museum. I was lucky enough to visit the famous historic site in Turkey just last month and this feels like the final piece of my Turkish trip. However, I have a little trouble locating it. It's housed within the Hofburg complex and I've seen photos of it. It's a pretty grand building. The trouble is, trying to find a grand building in Vienna is pretty hard because they're *all* grand.

I wander around, pretty sure I'm in the right area. I ask a couple of different people, but they don't know. Still, I have a hunch that it's just round the corner of the next very grand building.

My hunch proves right and, a few minutes later, I find that I have an entire museum to myself. Being part of the palace, the rooms are grand and spacious with sweeping staircases, marble columns and polished floors. I feel almost guilty having all this beauty to myself, but I enjoy the peace and the space as I look at the marvellous ancient statues and friezes. There are some beautiful details in the stonework and I spy a friendly goat nuzzling an angel, but it's the horses in the friezes that capture my attention – the fear in their eyes and the stretched nostrils. They're rearing and shying away from the war going on around them. They did not choose this life – or death – for themselves. I remember the Lipizzaners at the Spanish Riding School this morning. For centuries, man and horse have worked together. But what do the horses really make of that forced relationship?

By the time I return to my hotel, I have seen so many wonderful and varied things – both art and animal – I feel truly blessed and thankful that I have allowed myself three gloriously full days to explore this city. There's still so much more I'd like to see but, although I'm staying in Vienna tomorrow, I will be visiting another capital city entirely – by boat!

The Boisterous Boat to Bratislava

When I was researching places to see in Vienna, I discovered that day trips to Austria's neighbour Slovakia were popular. In particular, the boat trip to Bratislava. How exciting, I thought – to go from one European capital to another by boat in just over an hour.

I booked my ticket for 12.30 p.m.

This means that, on the morning of the boat trip, I have time to have breakfast at Café Sperl – the location of my favourite scene in *Before Sunrise* where Celine and Jesse 'ring' home without the use of phones. Alas, when I arrive, the table in the bay where the scene was shot is reserved. But I'm not going to miss my opportunity and ask a nearby customer if she could take a photo of me sitting there for the briefest moment.

After breakfast, I still have plenty of time before I have to catch the boat so I decide to try and find one more film location. It's funny when you picture something in your mind and then you're faced with a very different reality. That's what happens to me when I come out of the metro station. I'd imagined a stop on the outskirts of Vienna and a pleasant, easy walk to the bridge I'm trying to find. Instead, I find myself in a large shopping mall. This is a pretty major station with links to mainline trains and it takes me a while to find the right exit.

I'm not sure what happens, but I'm walking for ages. I have plenty of time so I'm not immediately worried, but it's going to be a long day and I won't be back at my hotel until after eight this evening.

I soon find myself in a beautiful residential area with elegant buildings with arched double doors leading into secret courtyards. I finally find the canal and I immerse myself in the moment. It's pleasant walking in the sunshine and there is elderflower in bloom, but I feel like I've gone out of my way a little and I'm not sure how long it's going to take me to walk to where the boat trip departs from. But, at least by walking, I won't have to get on the metro again.

At long last, I find the bridge used in the film. It's unmistakable and I'd love to walk across it and get some better photos, but I'm torn now. I know I'm pretty close to where I have to catch the boat, but I haven't actually found the exact place yet and have to check in.

So I decide not to walk across the bridge. It's frustrating to be so close, but I daren't be late for the boat.

As it turns out, the boat is late and there's a lot of hanging around. I queue to check in, but I'm told by the man at reception that I have the ticket on my phone. I ask if the return ticket is there and he checks. It is. But, when I try to find it myself, I can't. I hand my phone back to him, feeling rather useless, but he can't find it either now. I ask if he can print the tickets out for me to save me from panicking for the rest of the day that I won't be allowed to board the boat back to Vienna. It's one of my major worries when travelling alone – accessing tickets on my phone.

After my lengthy walk to get here in the sun, I'm pretty stressed. I am, in fact, almost on the verge of returning to my hotel and reassessing the day when a large stag party arrives. They're carrying cans and shot glasses and are in fancy costume, and they soon form a conga line, singing and jeering loudly.

Another smaller, slightly quieter stag party arrives, all of the guys holding cans. There's a hen party too, but they're well behaved by comparison. I can't help wondering what I've let myself in for. Is Bratislava some sort of party town? It is Saturday, I remind myself – a day I normally do my best to spend at home.

I reach for my ear plugs.

The first part of the boat ride is a bit of a nightmare as I find myself sitting right in the middle of the loud stags. I try to escape out onto the deck at the back of the boat, but we're not allowed to be out there for the first quarter of an hour or so as we navigate our way through the city. However, as soon as the doors are open, people are on the move and I switch seats, choosing one on the other side of the boat and enjoying the river views. It is a beautiful ride and there's a fabulous view of Devin Castle which towers high above the River Danube on its rocky perch and marks the border with Slovakia.

I'm so glad I didn't forgo the boat trip. I'd been looking forward to it so much and, when I arrive in Bratislava, it reminds me of the town in *Chitty Chitty Bang Bang*. But it's Saturday in a capital and it's warm. I see a beautiful church and the famous bronze figure known as 'The Watcher' who peeks out from a manhole cover and is very characterful indeed. I then decide to prioritise lunch, choosing a pizzeria in one of the side streets. And here's an introvert dilemma for the day – do I eat inside or outside? The table outside is near the main street where people will be constantly passing close by – a very unnerving prospect. But, inside, there is music blaring and it's the writer's curse that I will focus on the words of the songs and not be able to tune them out. In the end, I choose inside, picking a corner seat with plenty of space around me.

In the afternoon, I take my time wandering the backstreets and finding shady places to sit and soak it all in. I am fast learning that it's crucial to pace myself. After all, I still have two major cities to come. But I make time to climb one of the towers for views over the heart of Bratislava.

I arrive back at the river in plenty of time for the return boat and I can see a group of people waiting so I know I'm in the right place. There are a few benches in the shade and I sit on one. And then a thought occurs to me: what would I have done if I'd missed the boat? I guess I'd have had to take the train back to Vienna or a taxi if that didn't work out. But I have to be back in Vienna to check out tomorrow and to catch my train to Salzburg.

I'm so busy pondering this imagined scenario that, when I next look up, the queue of people has vanished. I'm on my feet in an instant and jog along the pavement to see the last of the group lined up to get on the boat. I am literally the last passenger to board. That'll teach me! Speculating about missing the boat nearly resulted in me actually missing it.

The boat ride back is far more relaxed than the outward journey and, luckily, there are no stags or hens. When we dock in Vienna, I cross the busy road and find my way to the right place to catch the tram back to my hotel. The trick here, I remind myself, is to make sure I'm going in the right direction. I don't want to make a mistake at night. It's been a long day and I'm ready for the peace of my hotel room and a long soak in the bath.

On the Move

It's Sunday morning and the bells are ringing as I leave the Theaterhotel and walk in the sunshine, my backpack on. I arrive at Westbahnhof train station with ninety minutes to spare. I go to the ticket office to have my ticket checked. I'm good to go.

I find noisy places like train stations stressful so choose to wait outside in the sunshine. There's a little fountain and some random stone 'shapes' on which people are sitting. They're not quite benches and not quite sculpture, but they'll do to pass a little time and it's good to take my backpack off. There are two other solo women sitting with their luggage and I wonder whether to say hello, but perhaps they're welcoming this moment of peace and solitude as I am.

The train leaves on time and is clean and spacious, and it's easy to find my compartment and seat. It looks like the seat next to me is free too for the two-hour journey so I can spread out a bit. It's certainly a more more pleasant way to travel than by the budget airlines where there is little personal space.

I took some care choosing my seat. I'm upstairs – a treat that we're not afforded with our UK trains – and I'm opposite the luggage so I can keep an eye on my backpack. I also have a window seat.

It's a quiet journey. There's a group of young men in front of me playing cards together and a lady comes to collect rubbish – twice – during the journey. It's a really relaxing and lovely way to travel.

I've given myself permission to get a taxi to my accommodation in Salzburg as I don't fancy trying to find a private apartment by myself. It's much easier to hand the address to a driver although, when I do, there seems to be an issue getting to the side of town where I'm staying as there's been a marathon today and certain roads are closed. I'm certainly glad I didn't try to find the place on my own.

When I arrive, all my fears about not being able to find it or to work out how to get inside are put to rest as the door is actually open and the cleaner is there. I have no trouble using the key safe and everything is in order in the apartment. The lights work, it's clean and tidy and there are no bugs visible anywhere.

I haven't really planned anything for arrival day in Salzburg, but there are several hours of daylight left and I've plenty of energy and can't wait to explore so I set off in what I hope is the right direction. However, I soon realise that I'm climbing a hill in a residential area and, as beautiful as it is with pretty well-detached homes, it's obviously not the way into town. I ask a local who's out walking, only she doesn't speak much English, but she points in what I hope is the right direction.

It's just a couple of minutes later when I spot something a little surprising – a mountain. There's a mountain in between the place where I'm staying and the centre of town and the only way to get through it is via a very long tunnel. I wasn't expecting this. There was no information about it in the apartment and I feel a little anxious as I enter. It seems to stretch forever. It's lit, of course, and there are countless posters and glass cases highlighting local businesses. But there aren't many people around and, when the tunnel divides, I become anxious that I'll never find my way back. I make a solemn pact with myself that I will leave for my apartment *way* before darkness descends.

I exit the tunnel a few minutes later and find myself in a quiet part of town and it doesn't take me long to reach the pretty cemetery of St Peter's Abbey. I'm delighted to find that the *katakomben* – catacombs – are still open. I buy a ticket and climb the steep steps to a remarkable twelfth century chapel carved into the mountainside. It feels more like a cave than a chapel and the low lighting used gives it all quite an eerie feeling. Tiny windows look out onto the cemetery grounds below and the stunning Salzburg churches and the hills beyond.

It's a beautiful evening and I find an Italian restaurant and order pasta, sitting at a table on the pavement. Italian restaurants are always a good bet for vegetarians when travelling abroad, I find! A couple from the US is next to me and we soon fall into conversation. They're on their way to Prague. I'm fast learning that there is a popular circuit of the cities I'm visiting: Vienna, Salzburg, Bratislava and Budapest with the additions of Prague and Munich tagged on to the journey too. As we chat, they say that they have a friend whose husband used to travel for work all the time and didn't want to go abroad on holidays. When he died, she wouldn't go anywhere on her own and will now only go to places locally that he went to. I can't help feeling sad that she is limiting her life in this way and it makes me feel so lucky that I found the confidence to do a trip like this by myself.

There are, undoubtedly, many challenges when you're on your own. Indeed, I've had so many anxious moments today from leaving my hotel and crossing Vienna with my backpack, to catching a train to a new city, and then finding my way into town through the tunnels. But, as I sit in the sunshine eating fresh *penne arrabbiata*, chatting to fellow travellers and with the promise of a beautiful new city to explore, I know that the rewards far outweigh the challenges.

A New City to Explore

I feel a total sense of helplessness being in a new foreign city on my own and, on my first full day in Salzburg, it takes me a little while to leave the safety of my beautiful apartment where it would be so easy to hide all day, using the excuse that I have a pool here and deserve some downtime after a busy schedule in Vienna. But I want to see Salzburg and know that, if I can just get myself out of the front door, I'll be fine.

As in so many European cities these days, there are bicycles everywhere and I'm mindful crossing roads, remembering which way the traffic flows. What has been wonderful in Austria, though, is that cars actually stop at pedestrian crossings – unlike in Turkey. I smile as I remember what my G Adventures travel companion Ella said about Turkish pedestrian crossings being 'just a suggestion'.

I find a local supermarket and pick up some food as I plan to mostly self-cater while I'm here. Even the simplest of daily tasks provide a chance to learn. Not only is the card reader right at the end of the checkout where you pack your groceries, but you take your basket back to the entrance too. It's simple things that can quickly mark you out as a stranger in town.

I have sent a message to my host, Alex, asking how to get into town without going through the dreaded tunnels, and he tells me that there are three buses that will take me to the stop I want so I take one of those into town and find my way to the DomQuartier. I'm not too sure what's housed in this very grand building other than a set of curiosity cabinets full of little treasures that I'd love to see.

When I go to buy my ticket, I'm warned that the building is vast and it'll be over a kilometre's walk to see everything. This doesn't faze me. I walk a lot when I'm visiting new cities. It's always so easy to do when you're not actually thinking about walking but focused on all the wonderful things you're seeing.

I walk through some very grand state rooms with tall walls and impressive paintings on the ceilings. There are fabulous chandeliers and ornate mirrors which bounce the light around the room, and everything seems to be gilded – chairs, tables – even the stoves. And there are some fine portraits. The DomQuartier seems to be a wonderful mix of palace, art gallery and museum only without the crowds.

There is one marvellous moment when I open a door onto a roof terrace and see the looming façade of Saltzburg's cathedral. As I cross the terrace, I enjoy the views across the city's squares to the left and right and then enter the next door and find myself in the cathedral organ loft. It's a wonderful surprise and I wonder that there aren't more tourists here, but I'm not complaining because it's rather lovely not to be battling crowds.

The only thing is, I've been walking for some time now and haven't yet seen the very thing I came in for – the curiosity cabinets. I haven't missed a vital turn somewhere, have I? I suppose it would have been easy to do and I don't fancy retracing my steps as it's been a long walk to get to this point.

I find them right at the end of the tour. Housed in what looks like a passageway with ornate stucco ceilings and shiny red and white chequered marble flooring, it's an absolute delight. The seventeenth century cabinets are black with gold metal latticework across the front, and they contain all sorts of treasure both natural and man-made from seashells and coral to crucifixes and rosaries. Of course, it's the crystals that draw my attention – particularly a stunning clear quartz point placed on its own gilded plinth.

The DomQuartier has been a total joy. I think that can happen when you do a minimal amount of research into a place – just enough to know what your options are, but not too exhaustive so that it still comes as a delightful surprise.

***

The afternoon sky is looking pretty stormy as I take the funicular to Salzburg's fortress. After the peace of the DomQuartier, I find the fortress busy and noisy and I move through the rooms quickly. I sit in one of the courtyards with my picnic, gazing up at the darkening sky and wondering if we're going to see lightning. It would be a dramatic setting, but there is nothing but the subdued distant rumble of thunder. I wonder if my father came here when he visited Salzburg in the nineties. I recently found a photo album from his trip. Of course, his focus had been very much on Mozart and there are several pictures of the Mozart museum. I find myself smiling as I remember his love of Mozart's piano concertos and how we would

listen to them together and test each other to see if we could guess the precise moment when the piano would come in. I wonder what Dad's response would be if he knew that the main inspiration for my visit to Salzburg is *The Sound of Music* rather than Mozart. I think he might forgive me although he wouldn't be too amused by my personal renaming of the Mozart Bridge as the 'Do Re Mi' Bridge.

After returning to the town via the funicular, I indulge in a bit of chocolate shopping and treat myself to a couple as I sit by the impressive Baroque horse pond – one of the locations used in *The Sound of Music*. It's one of the joys of travelling when you stumble upon locations like this that are so familiar to you from the world of film and then they're suddenly right in front of you. It never fails to make me smile. I walk home through the tunnels, grateful that I find my way without getting horribly lost and, perhaps, a little less afraid of them now than yesterday.

My confidence is building. Maria von Trapp would be proud of me.

The Sound of Music

It's the day I've been so looking forward to – *The Sound of Music* tour. The coach leaves at 9.15 a.m. near the Mirabell Gardens – a part of Salzburg I haven't yet seen so I'm anxious to get there in plenty of time.

When I get on the bus into town, I double check with the driver.

'Mirabell?' I ask and he nods. I place my money on a little shelf but the driver points to what I'm sure is a hole on a level above so I put my coins in there.

'*No!*' he cries and he proceeds to lift the whole unit up to retrieve my coins. Luckily, he looks amused. It's obvious that nobody has ever tried to put their coins down *this* hole before. I apologise profusely.

'Well, you've definitely got them!' I say and he's smiling. I'm relieved that he has a sense of humour. 'I'll know for next time,' I say. 'Only, I'm leaving tomorrow!'

I sit down as the bus pulls away, wondering how many passengers have witnessed my antics.

When we reach my destination on the other side of the Salzach river, I leave the bus by the middle door and I'm sorry not to pass the driver since I wanted to thank him. As I make my way to where my tour leaves, I turn around to see the bus pulling out and the driver waves at me, a huge smile on his face. I wave back, laughing.

As ever, I'm horribly early. The plus side of this is that I cross the road and wander through the park and have a genuinely gorgeous moment of surprise when I recognise the entrance to the Mirabell Gardens and the steps from the end of the 'Do Re Mi' song.

I find the park toilet. It's fifty cents. I use my one and only coin which, in half an hour's time, I regret as I'd really like to go again before getting on the coach as there's no telling how long it'll be until a comfort stop.

I stop two women and ask if they have any change. They don't. I then spot a building which looks like some kind of conference centre and decide to try my luck. There are plenty of people coming and going and I hope there isn't a strict security system. I stride in confidently but slowly enough to try and spot where a toilet might be. Beside the stairs, I clock a plan of the building. The toilets are on the next floor.

When I get there, I see that there are stalls set up and people in crisp shirts and muted-coloured jackets. In my pink dress and stripy hat, I do rather stand out. I move quickly. When I come to leave the building, I see there's an escalator so decide to take that – meeting a man at the top who pauses and smiles. For a split second, I think he's going to challenge me as to why I'm there, but he simply gestures for me to go first. It's a relief to get outside once again and I can't help but feel sorry for the conference folk stuck indoors on this glorious day when I'm about to explore the locations where *The Sound of Music* was filmed.

And there's no mistaking the Panorama Tours' coach when it turns up. It's bright red and has Julie Andrews as Maria, and the von Trapp children emblazoned on its side. It's wonderful and I'm so excited.

The coach driver is singing 'Do Re Mi' as people board.

'You're warming us up!' I tell him.

'It's my favourite film,' he replies. I guess it would have to be.

I choose a seat fairly close to the front of the coach. Everyone is in couples or small family groups and I wonder if there'll be another solo traveller who will sit next to me. Sure enough, there is. Her name is Amy and she's an oceanography graduate, looking to enter into teaching in that field. She's travelling around Europe and is excited to do this tour as her parents did it many years ago.

Our guide is warm, knowledgeable and enthusiastic. I can't help wondering how many times he's shared the same stories from behind the scenes and how many times he's sung the songs from the film.

We see so many locations including Leopoldskron Palace – the house whose garden was used and the lake beyond where the boat capsized throwing Maria and all the children into the water. We see the pretty summer house used in the 'Sixteen Going on Seventeen' song in the grounds of Hellbrun Palace. Then we have a stop in Mondsee to see the church where they filmed the wedding scene. And we see some fabulous Austrian lakes and mountains, watch clips from the film and sing a few songs.

When we return to Salzburg, our guide finishes the tour in the Mirabell Gardens – a key location in the film and where much of the 'Do Re Mi' song and dance was shot. There's a young woman in our group wearing a pretty white dress with a sky-blue ribbon around her waist. It strikes me as a quirky choice, but it isn't until I remember the line from the song 'Favourite Things' that I realise the significance. 'Girls in white dresses with blue satin sashes'.

I point this out to Amy and we strike up a conversation with the girl and have our photo taken together in front of the Pegasus fountain. I ask how she came to be a fan of the film and she said she's a relative newcomer – falling in love with it during repeat viewings in lockdown. We talk about our travels and, like me, she confesses to arriving at train stations at least an hour early.

It's a little sad to say goodbye to my two *Sound of Music* friends, but we all split up after the tour and I decide to stay on this side of the river for the afternoon, finding somewhere for lunch.

I listen to an American couple in their sixties sitting to my right, and hear that they met in the 90s and have been married for thirty years. I'm fascinated that they talk to each other – *really* talk – like good friends. There are no awkward pauses or silences and neither does so much as glance at a phone. They are fully present with each other in that moment – sharing a leisurely lunch together in the sunshine in a foreign city.

Towards the end of my lunch, the man admires my amethyst pendant and we chat. They are in Europe for two weeks and travel by public transport whenever they can. They've just been to Budapest by train – my very journey tomorrow.

After lunch, I try and find a cemetery I've read about only I'm not really having much luck. It's hot and I'm pretty tired so I just sort of drift in what I hope is the right direction. In one of those wonderful serendipitous moments, I stumble upon a completely different cemetery – St Sebastian's – which is even better than the one I'd been trying to find as it houses the mausoleum of Prince Archbishop Wolf Dietrich – a character whose name keeps popping up in the history of Salzburg.

The mausoleum is a round building with a domed roof set in a beautiful graveyard which is the resting place not only of Wolf Dietrich but members of Mozart's family too. I dare to take a peep through the barred doorway into the mausoleum. It feels very M R James to me and just a little bit spooky on this sunny day.

I walk around the stunning Rococo portal and sit in the shade taking it all in. I love moments like these – making unexpected and wonderful discoveries. It feels like I've stumbled into a secret world that I'm not meant to be in at all. But there's still somewhere else I'm hoping to find today, only it's on the other side of the river which means a long walk in the warm afternoon.

The road by the river seems noisy so I decide to walk along the next one back that runs parallel to it – which makes all the difference. Not only is it much quieter – it's also beautiful with quirky buildings and a chance to see how the locals live as I spy people coming and going, briefly glimpsing rooms and staircases through open doors.

I spot a bookshop and venture inside. There's a cocker spaniel in a basket under the desk and chairs are being assembled for a meeting. The owner smiles and nods and I wish I knew a few words of German because it's a lovely scene and feels so welcoming. I wish I could stay, but I need to keep moving.

I'm heading to another location from *The Sound of Music* – Nonnberg Abbey – and it's quite a climb to get there but, like everywhere that's a climb in Salzburg, it's worth it and I find that I have the place to myself. Although they weren't allowed to film inside the building itself, there were a few shots of the abbey grounds and it's the gate at the main entrance through which Maria leaves and starts singing my favourite song from the film, 'I Have Confidence'. So I'm very excited to walk through this gate now myself. What's even more exciting is that the abbey is open to visitors. I hadn't expected this extra treat.

It's cool and my eyes take a moment to adjust after the bright sunshine. There is some kind of singing playing over a sound system but it keeps cutting out. Still, I can tell it's not Rodgers and Hammerstein.

I sit for a little while and think about the real Maria who was a novice at this abbey. I wonder what she thought about her representation on film and the legions of fans who followed in its wake.

It's still so warm and sunny as I leave the abbey and I don't quite want to return to my apartment yet so I pop into a bakery and choose a Viennese finger, eating it at a table outside which overlooks the square with a fine view of the cathedral. Salzburg really is a gem of a city and I've loved my time here. My exploration has been a little less hectic than in Vienna because it's a much smaller city to navigate and I've found it easier to get around on foot. My three nights have been just perfect.

And now I've another three nights awaiting me in another city – if I can find my way there.

Budapest

I'm a little sad to be leaving my apartment. It's been nice to have this homely base, but it's time to move on. Moving on is something I'm almost getting used to now and I think I'm actually getting quite good at organising my laundry, arranging my packing cubes and sorting my backpack.

I've left everything clean and tidy in the apartment, checking to make sure I've not left anything in the wardrobe or fridge, leaving my city tax money in the envelope provided and leaving the key in the apartment as requested.

There are at least three different buses to the train station from my part of town so I've no excuse not to catch one. I'll save the taxi ride for when I get to Budapest.

Salzburg to Budapest takes around six hours by train. Once again, I arrive an hour early at the station and the train is running half an hour late. I've booked the Quiet Carriage and the seat next to me is free to begin with, a young gentleman sitting there after the half-way point.

As the train arrives in Vienna, it starts to get noisy with a group boarding with massive suitcases. They struggle to fit them into the luggage compartment. There's a lot of pushing and pulling. I glance up at my neat backpack on the top shelf and it looks tiny by comparison, and I'm so glad that I've embraced travelling light.

But I have an even closer encounter with luggage as I'm leaving the train. There's a man with two huge cases just ahead of me and he swings one up and knocks my leg without even knowing he's done it. He sighs and groans and looks out of the doors impatiently as the train comes into the station, asking me if I know which door will open. When the door to the left finally opens, he takes one of his cases, climbs down the steps and promptly falls on top of it as he stumbles.

I'm rather glad to leave the chaos of the train behind but I have my first Hungarian test awaiting me at the ATM. I need to get some forints and didn't work out ahead how many I might need so I get my phone out, realising that I'm holding people up. I chastise myself for being so disorganised.

Forints safely stashed in my money belt, I catch a taxi from outside the station and it's a pretty hairy ride through the city. At one point, we almost crash into a bus and I'm pretty sure it isn't the bus driver's fault. But I arrive at the Cortile Hotel in one piece and I'm greeted by the lovely Lola on reception.

There is probably time to explore a little but the long train journey and scary taxi ride have left me pretty depleted. Instead, I make myself comfortable in my beautiful room, shower and change into my swimsuit. I then take the lift up to the rooftop where there's an infinity pool with views across the city to St Stephen's Basilica.

I love how the last part of my journey has brought me to Budapest with a glorious pool to enjoy and some of the most famous spas in Europe. And I fully intend to enjoy them all.

Navigating Alone

On my first morning in Budapest, I have planned to visit the famous Széchenyi baths. Lola on reception directs me to the metro, telling me that it's very straightforward to use. I leave the hotel for the first time, careful to take my bearings, remembering names of shops and each new road I cross.

The metro is easy to find as it's by the opera house and I walk down the steps into the station. I see a man in a little booth and decide to get my ticket from him. Unfortunately, he doesn't sell tickets. He also tells me that I need to be on the other platform for Széchenyi. I thank him and then look around the station, wondering how I get to the other platform. It doesn't seem obvious so I go back to the man in little booth. He tells me I have to leave the station and cross the road. I do this, waiting at traffic lights to cross the very busy road and I then make my way down the steps onto the platform where there is a ticket machine. I tap my card against it but nothing comes out despite a green tick being clearly displayed. I try again. And again. But no ticket comes out. I'm beginning to panic. Have I bought a ticket? I don't want to get on a train and be challenged to produce a ticket. If it's anything like Vienna and I'm stopped without a physical ticket, I could be in for a hefty fine.

A train pulls in and I almost grab hold of the first woman who gets off. She is very sweet and offers to help me, but she says I really need to download an app on my phone. She does her best to navigate me through this, but then she has to leave and I'm left feeling stranded with a message on my phone saying that I need to create a password or some such nonsense. I'm nearly in tears at this stage. Should it really be this hard to travel a few stops on the metro? And it's also time-consuming. I'm getting nowhere and so I decide to plead with the man in the booth for help.

This, of course, means leaving the station and crossing the road again to reach the other platform. When I get there, I notice a large ticket machine and give that a go, but get absolutely nowhere with it so I approach the man in the booth once again. What's his job if not to help a struggling Englishwoman on her first day in Budapest? Rather reluctantly, it seems to me, he leaves the safety of his booth and, when I tell him that I tried to purchase tickets with my card, he asks me to tap my card on the machine.

'You have three tickets,' he tells me.

'I do?'

He nods, telling me that I don't need a physical ticket. I am ready for my journey. I sigh in both relief and exasperation. Of course, I have to leave the platform and cross the road again to catch the next train. When I get to the platform, I see a group of about ten people crowded round the little machine that I was struggling to use just minutes before. Four of them are American gentleman in their sixties. I can't help but smile and quickly tell them that they just need to tap their card to pay and, no, they will not receive a printed ticket.

'It's not intuitive, is it?' one of the gentlemen tells me.

'No. I've just spent twenty minutes trying to work it out,' I confess.

It's such a relief to not be the only one to find these things a challenge and I'm so happy to have been able to help this group on their way. We board the next train together and I sit with the Americans and chat to one who tells me they're travelling around Europe together. It sounds like a fascinating trip and I'd love to talk to them more but we part ways outside the station at Széchenyi, wishing each other good luck with our journeys. I just love how travel gifts you with these fleeting meetings and little insights into people's lives.

I go into the baths via the smaller entrance nearest the metro station. This is the kind of excursion that makes me very nervous as there are so many things I don't know. The pricing, for example. There seem to be a lot of different tickets as far as I could tell from looking online. You can book for a changing room or private cubicle, I think. But how does it work? Where do you go? How do the lockers work? And what can you take inside? Can you carry a bag with your towel and a drink? I've remembered to bring my own towel and a bathing cap as well so I can swim in the main pool outside. Usually, all these unknown variables would put me off ever coming to a place like this, but it does look rather special and I am looking forward to enjoying the warmth of the thermal water.

I buy my ticket without any problems. It seems that I can't pay for a private cubicle from this entrance so I'm not too sure if I'll be in a communal changing area. I'm given a wristband which will work the locker and find my way to a row of wooden doors. When I look inside, it isn't a changing cubicle at all and I can see right through to the lockers where a crowd of people are. I look back the way I've come, confused, and a man comes forward to show me how things work, ushering me back into a cubicle which I don't believe to be a cubicle. He leans across and closes a door, shutting out my view of the lockers, then he pulls down a piece of wood which acts like a bench, demonstrating that, when I close the door by which I entered, the bench acts as a lock between the two doors. Ingenious! I don't think I would have ever worked it out for myself though.

Once changed and having successfully worked out the locker system, I make my way outside to the grand courtyard where there are three enormous pools. I'm wearing my brand-new bathing cap so I can do lengths in the proper grown-up pool first. It's probably the biggest pool I've ever swum in and it isn't too busy compared to the other pools. I do a few lengths and then get into the Adventure Pool which has a fun whirlpool at its centre which catches you up in its current and carries you around. Everybody is smiling. It's impossible not too – it's the kind of thing that turns grown-ups into kids in mere seconds.

After this, I venture into the Thermal Pool which feels like stepping into a bath. Indeed, there's a notice suggesting you spend no longer than twenty minutes in it as it's so warm. But what a joy it is to relax here, gazing up at the yellow Neo-Baroque building of the bath complex. Opened in 1913, it's one of the largest and grandest baths in Europe and I can see why it attracts so many people.

It's a little chilly when I get out of the Thermal Pool even though the sun is shining. I decide to explore the indoor pools and find myself in a corridor where the private cubicles are. And it's here that I hear a voice.

'Hello? Helloooo?'

I ignore it at first, imagining it's a chap calling out to a mate in an adjoining cubicle. But it continues.

'Hello?'

And it's joined by a female voice.

'Is there anyone there?'

I approach the voices and, as I turn a corner, I spot the head of a young man craning over the top of a cubicle door.

'Are you okay?' I ask, assuming he's English.

'We're locked in!' he says, the head of his female companion now appearing alongside him. 'Can you help?' He passes his wrist band down to me from the gap above the door and I swipe it in front of the lock on my side, assuming this is how it works. Luckily, the door unlocks and the two young people emerge. I don't ask them how long they've been stuck in there, but we all laugh together at the predicament now that it's resolved.

'You certainly deserve a relaxing soak after that!' I tell them and I can't stop smiling at all the little adventures I seem to be having when travelling on my own.

I spend a little while going from pool to pool inside the complex, but I'm finding it noisy and there are chipped floor tiles and it's all a bit grubby. When I see a lady coming out of the loo without washing her hands, I decide it's time to go, but it isn't easy finding my way to the exit and I go round in circles for a good long time before finding my locker. I can now operate the changing room door and, as I catch the metro back, I can't help feeling a little smug that I now know how to use it.

I make my way back to my hotel to drop my swimming bag off, smiling at the morning's events – the endless crossing of the road trying to work out how to use the metro, helping the Americans and rescuing a couple from a cubicle. These are all things that only happened because I dared to venture out into the world. Little adventures – just waiting for me to find them.

***

In the afternoon, as I walk towards the city centre, I pass St Stephen's Basilica and hesitate. I had made a note to visit this on my last morning in Budapest as my flight isn't until the afternoon and it's easy to get to from my hotel. However, I'm here now, and I'm a great believer in making the most of opportunities that hand themselves to me so easily. But how do I get a ticket? It's quickly apparent that I can't get one at the actual entrance so I walk around. I walk *right* around – following the signs which take me to the back of the basilica. So where now? The board in front of me points to the right but there's nothing there. I try not to panic. People – lots of people – are working this out every day. If they didn't, the basilica wouldn't have any paying visitors, would it? So I pause, take a breath and look around. It's then that I spot a row of shops accessible by a flight of steps and, amongst them, one which is selling tickets to the basilica. It could have been made easier to spot, I think, but at least I've found

it now. I have to wonder, though – is it just me that finds everyday things like this such a challenge? Or is it because I haven't travelled – or even been out of my own village much over the years? I'm quickly finding that travelling on your own means you're constantly solving problems.

St Stephen's Basilica is named in honour of the first King of Hungary and there's a much-revered relic housed here – his mummified hand. Known as the Holy Right Hand, it's one of the strangest things I've ever seen. You can clearly see each finger clenched into an eternal fist and it's obviously very precious to the Roman Catholic church as it's held in a double reliquary – bejewelled and beautiful.

After leaving the basilica, I cross the Danube river over the Chain Bridge adorned with fierce lions. The river divides the two districts of Buda and Pest, and I'm heading to the funicular on the Buda side of the city. I will then make my way to Fisherman's Bastion – a famous viewpoint. I'm also hoping to see beautiful St Matthias. When I arrive, there's a queue for tickets for the cathedral so I walk around first, taking photos of the parliament building on the Pest side, which looks glorious even on this cloudy grey day.

I then return to get a ticket for St Matthias but the kiosk now seems to be shut. I hasten to the church door, but the woman standing guard tells me it's now closed. I frown. It's 4.15 p.m. I ask if I can just cross to the next door and peep inside.

'I've come all the way from England,' I try. But she's having none of it.

'I want to go home,' she retorts and there's no arguing with that.

It's disappointing as I don't really have time to return here another day, but I decide to wander the backstreets instead. I find a curious museum. It seems to be a dungeon and I take a leaflet which declares it's 'Europe's 8th most popular tourist attraction'. But there's nobody here. I doubt if it's even Budapest's 8th most popular attraction. Still, it's tempting, but there's something holding me back. I'm not sure how scary it will be with it being a dungeon and, apparently, the place where Vlad the Impaler was held, but what I'm most scared of is being the only tourist down there if there's an enthusiastic curator who hasn't had anyone to talk to all day. I might never get out again. So I return the leaflet and walk away.

I retrace my steps – taking the funicular down the hill and walking across the Chain Bridge and then I follow the river to Parliament. I find the iron shoes – a poignant memorial erected in 2005 in memory of the Hungarian Jews who were shot on the banks of the Danube by Arrow Cross militiamen in 1944–45. It's a moving sight and some people have lit candles and placed white feathers inside the shoes.

    I sit on a bench overlooking the river for a while. From this vantage point, I can see the route I walked across the bridge and on to Fisherman's Bastion and back again. I must have covered quite a few miles today and I'm not done yet as I have to find my way back to my hotel. But I have one of those surreal moments where I can't quite believe where I am… sitting on the banks of the Danube in Budapest – a city in a part of Europe I've never been to before and, like all the places I've visited on my trip so far, I feel so grateful to be seeing it.

Final Day Fatigue

Friday marks my last day in Budapest and the final day of my trip. It's raining and my eyes are sore. I feel headachy, but it's probably just tiredness. I nearly lose my nerve and almost don't leave the hotel, but then I think of Carla – my friend from the Turkey trip – and how she told me she doesn't want to spend any longer than she has to in a 'sterile room' – she wants to be out seeing and doing things! So I muster up my willpower to leave the safety of the hotel. I should be feeling courageous by now – this is my fourth city on the trip – but I'm flagging a little.

I pop by reception to book my transfer for the airport tomorrow, hoping to see Lola, but she's helping somebody else so I talk to her colleague and she makes the booking for me. As this is being processed, Lola becomes free so I take the opportunity to ask where the boat trips go from and she kindly books me a ticket and circles my map to show me where to get on. A boat trip seems like just the right choice today. It leaves from a part of the river I've not walked to yet – just beyond the Chain Bridge but, as I approach, I find that there's a tramline between me and the river and I have to walk quite a distance before I can cross both it and the road safely.

There are only three of us on board for the ride down the Danube, but more join when the boat pulls up at Margaret Island. I'm tempted to get off and have a look around, but the sky is threatening rain so I stay onboard. The view of Parliament is stunning from the water even under a grey sky.

There's just one more thing I want to do before trying to find somewhere for lunch – the Ferris wheel. Located in a park close to the river, it's easy to find and very quiet when I get there. There are forty-two cabins so I get one to myself. It's a little unnerving as it's partially open to the elements and I later read that it's the largest Ferris wheel in Europe. There are raindrops on the cabin and it's swaying quite a bit, but the speed is gentle and the views of St Stephen's Basilica and across the river are wonderful.

When I come back down to earth, I try to find somewhere to eat, but I'm not having any luck. I pop into one small café and ask what salads they do. The lady points to the board on the wall. There are salads with coriander. Salads with syrup. Salads with meat. And she's hovering over me. I nod politely and leave. Lunch can wait until dinner. I need to hide in my room for a while.

I try not to feel guilty about heading back to my hotel. After all, I'm paying to stay in a pretty nice place – it would be a shame not to make the most of it, so I have a rest and go up to the rooftop for a swim. It feels rather luxurious to be swimming in the middle of the afternoon, but it's a good choice because it's really clouded over now and looks like it could rain.

Sure enough, as soon as I leave the hotel to go in search of food in the evening, the heavens open and the rain is soon bouncing off the pavements. I take shelter under one of the umbrellas of an eatery. A woman is standing under the adjacent one and motions for me to join her. She is Kurdish and works sixteen hours a day at the eatery. She tells me that stormy weather like this is typical of Budapest and I say that I'm used to the rain being British. It's a lovely shared moment as the traffic splashes through the wet streets and pedestrians hurry by with wet feet.

It's a relief to get out of the rain a few minutes later when I find somewhere to eat. I feel as if I haven't really done Budapest justice today but, at the same time, I know I've done all I could without pushing my energy levels. Like my time in Istanbul, I feel saturated by city life. It's definitely time to go home.

The Cat Café

On the final morning of my trip, I have time for one more little adventure. When I was researching things to do in Budapest, I discovered that there was a cat café. I'd never heard of such a thing, but it is apparently *a thing* so I go to investigate.

There are fifteen cats at the cat café and they're free to roam, sleep and play wherever the fancy takes them, and it's very amusing to see some of them making themselves quite at home on tables and chairs. There are even sofas in a back room and high-rise baskets.

The service is slow, but I don't have to check out of my hotel for several hours so what nicer place could there be than sitting here, thinking about the incredible trip I've had. I've spent such a large portion of my life shutting myself away, filtering things out and focusing on details. But now I want to open up and venture out – discover new places and meet new people. And I'm so proud of what I've achieved – personally – on this trip. I've stayed in a hostel for the first time in over thirty years, I flew into one city and I'm about to fly back home from another. I worked out how to use metros, trams, buses and boats. I arranged two train journeys to new cities and I checked in to four different accommodations including an apartment with a contactless key lock. I also met the most wonderful people. I even managed to help a few of them as others helped me in turn and that feels like such a beautiful thing to be a part of.

Getting lost and going wrong still makes me feel deeply uncomfortable. But I'm not travelling to feel comfy, I guess. I can find plenty of comfort at home. Travel is about getting out of your comfort zone and growing, learning and – dare I say – *blossoming* when you do.

Lessons Learned in Austria, Slovakia and Hungary

- Be kind to yourself when you've gone wrong. Accept it; it's fine. The only person you have to worry about is you and you are doing okay. You'll find your way and, when you do, you'll be so proud of yourself because *you* worked out how to do it.

- Ask a person in uniform. On my trip, I reached out to and was helped by an Austrian pilot, an official from the Colombian embassy and a policeman. Dog walkers usually know an area well so are good to ask. Shopkeepers too.

- Use Google Translate on food labels. I bought what I thought was strawberry-centred chocolate. It was, indeed, strawberry, but I overlooked that 'pepper' was also a key ingredient!

- And remember – very few, if any, of your fears will actually materialis. Losing keys to apartments, getting lost in a new city, missing trains, hotels not knowing anything about your reservation – these were just a few of the worries I carried with me. Okay, I kind of got lost a couple of times, but I was generally heading in the right direction and I always found my way… in the end!

I Dream of Italy

What is it about Italy that captivates so many of us?

In 1994, Roy and I took – not a gap year – but a gap month. I'd just left a job that I couldn't get away from fast enough, and Roy was owed some leave, so it seemed like the perfect opportunity to have an adventure together. I was desperate to see Italy; Roy wanted to see Switzerland. So we compromised and booked three weeks in Italy and one in Switzerland. Well, you can't have *fewer* than three weeks in Italy, can you? We booked a coach tour: 'Highlights of Italy' which picked us up in Venice, took us to Assisi, Florence, Pisa, Sienna, Rome, Sorrento and a few other places in between. It was a dreamy trip and it scratched a lot of itches.

Roy and I had our honeymoon in Positano on the glorious Amalfi coast and we've had a few trips to Venice over the years and, as soon as I got my travelling mojo back in 2023, I knew I wanted to see more so I booked a week in Sicily with my brother. I knew there was more exploring to do in mainland Italy – *much* more! But where to choose? What would make a good solo trip?

I've heard many positive things about the city of Bologna. Famous in writer circles as the host city for the Children's Book Fair, it's been on my radar for many years, but what excites me the most is its rail links to the many other northern Italian cities I've always wanted to see. So, one day during the summer, I take a deep breath and book nine nights in Bologna for September, determining to use this beautiful city as a base from which to explore others in the region from Florence in the south and Verona, Padua, Mantua and others to the north.

This will be a slightly shorter trip than my Vienna/Salzburg/Budapest one and I won't be moving accommodation as I did there, so I keep telling myself it will be less exhausting. I will be catching different trains almost every day and that has me a little concerned, but this is going to be a super-cultural trip with cathedrals, palaces and baptisteries galore, so I know it'll be worth any stress I might encounter when it comes to working out the train stations… won't it?

The Testing Travel Day

My first train of the trip is one I've been looking forward to: the monorail from Bologna airport. When I follow the signs to it, I notice that the escalators are roped off so I take the stairs, grateful that I'm travelling light. I pass the ticket machines because I know you can pay by contactless card at the barrier. But, when I reach them, they're roped off too. I look around and see a young woman is heading down a spiral metal staircase so perhaps I'm in the wrong place. I decide to follow her and find myself on a road where the buses leave from. This can't be right.

I turn back and head up the spiral stairs, my suitcase now feeling a little heavier than before. I walk past the roped-off barriers, back to the ticket machine area where I remember seeing a member of staff. There is a group of travellers around him and I soon discover that the monorail is not working. I'll have to take a bus into town. This takes a little bit of working out, but I manage it with the help of another young traveller. Of course, it means retracing my steps and going back down the spiral stairs and out onto the road.

This has been an exhausting arrival and I still have the walk from the train station. But I'm so proud of myself for getting on the bus with the other tourists. I haven't wimped out and hopped into a nice easy taxi. I'm saving money taking the local transport and it makes me feel like a real traveller.

The trouble is, the bus doesn't stop in front of the train station as I'd imagined and I have a panicky few moments as I try to work out where I am. Somehow, I navigate my way across a busy road and soon see a roundabout which leads me to the bed and breakfast where I'm staying.

It's a rather unattractive building and I'm not really sure what to expect so I approach the porter and he tells me I need to get the lift to the seventh floor. I've had no written instructions to tell me this and so it takes me by surprise. At least the lift is working; I'm not sure I could have faced any more stairs today. But there's a brief moment when I fear the lift is stuck as I reach the seventh floor and the door doesn't open. It takes me a second to realise that it's actually opened behind me. I take a breath, allowing myself some space for rookie mistakes on travel day.

I walk out onto the landing to discover two doors. One of them has a sign for the bed and breakfast and there are three keypads and an intercom, but I haven't been sent a code. The door is firmly locked against me and there is no answer when I press the intercom several times. I pull my printed instructions from my handbag. I had an email saying that somebody would meet me and I gave my rough arrival time. But it's clear there is nobody here.

I ring the phone number I've been given but it doesn't work. I'm seriously panicking now so I dare to ring the bell of the private flat next door to the bed and breakfast. Luckily, an elderly man answers and helps me with the phone number and I finally get through to someone.

'When are you arriving?' the man on the phone asks.

'I'm here now.'

'I'll be there in ten minutes.'

What a relief! And it's even more of a relief when he opens the door – without actually being there – and I'm able to sit in an air-conditioned reception area. The whole experience of finding and getting into this place has left me shaken and I firmly tell myself that I will book nothing but hotels from now on when solo travelling because hotel doors are always open and there are staff available to welcome you. Of course, when the wonderful Francesco arrives to welcome me, all my anxiety evaporates and I feel instantly at ease.

After unpacking, I can't resist walking into town as there are still several hours of daylight and I can't wait to see Bologna's Piazza Maggiore. My first view of the *Due Torri* – the Two Towers – is breathtaking. I had hoped to climb the taller one – the Asinelli – but I quickly learn that the shorter – the Garisenda – is being restored. It's leaning at an alarming angle, more so than the famous Leaning Tower of Pisa, and so the whole area has been closed off to the public. It's hard to believe that there were many more towers like this in Bologna with wealthy families vying with each other to build the tallest. The city would have looked like a medieval Manhattan.

As I continue to walk, I see that there are restaurants lining most of the narrow streets, just leaving a slither in between for pedestrians. Bologna is thought by many to be the food capital of Italy and I can see how it got one of its nicknames: *La Grassa* – the fat one.

Unfortunately, the next morning, I'm in for a disappointing first foodie experience in Bologna. I've been given nine plastic cards to hand over at a bar in the street below my accommodation in exchange for breakfast. Each card is printed with the word *Colazione* and I'm looking forward to my first breakfast. I've even learned the phrase for scrambled eggs in Italian. The picture on each of the cards depicts a croissant and a cup of coffee and I soon discover that that is, in fact, all you get for breakfast at the bar. I enquire about eggs or fruit or even a smoothie. The man behind the counter shakes his head.

'This isn't an English breakfast,' he says, firmly putting me in my place.

I guess I'll have to look for sustenance elsewhere throughout my stay in *La Grassa*.

When You Have Nobody to Please but Yourself

I have always longed to see Verona and decide to make this destination top of my list. I've done a lot of research before my trip and all the vloggers say how cheap rail travel is. But my return ticket to Verona is nearly forty pounds. Still, I'm not going to come all this way and not visit one of the most beautiful cities in Italy. So I book my ticket at one of the machines at the station and it's an exciting moment as I navigate my way down into the subterranean levels of Bologna's train station.

I have a little time before my train and see a booking officer at a counter near my platform so I ask if I can book a ticket to Florence for the next day. I blanch when she tells me the price. It's even more expensive than my Verona ticket, but she assures me it's cheaper to book it today than tomorrow and I go ahead. I decide I'll have to get organised for the week and book as much as I can in advance.

The *Frecciarossa* – literally "Red Arrow" – to Verona is a lovely smooth ride and a highlight is when we cross the Po – the longest river in Italy. But things aren't so relaxing when I actually arrive and find out that it's two kilometres into town and I don't know the way. It's also quite hot and I don't want to expend excess energy walking along busy streets before my day of sightseeing has even begun. Luckily, I'm given help getting a bus ticket into town by the locals, but I'm aware I'm making myself vulnerable with my credit card on display and it's a relief when I finally make it into town.

After my rather meagre breakfast, I find a café and buy myself a large fruit smoothie, sitting down and just taking in the fact that I have made it to Italy on my own and that I have a full day ahead of me in the sunshine to explore this beautiful place. It's twenty-six degrees and I'll have to pace myself but, with it being my first day, I'm so excited to jump right in and see as much as I can. This time in Italy is all about beauty. I want to see the most beautiful buildings and the most stunning art, and the joy of travelling solo is that I can indulge that passion while not boring anybody else. I can take my time and savour every little moment.

So I make my way to the largest church, St Anastasia, and lose myself in the beauty of it all before drifting around some of the backstreets in search of lunch. I always try to avoid main squares and the most bustling of streets when I choose a lunch spot, and it pays off when I find a delightful restaurante which fills my plate with vegetarian goodies from their buffet-style bar. It fuels me for an afternoon of exploration and I take a walk along the Adige River, cross the Castelvecchio Bridge and make my way to the Arena di Verona – the enormous amphitheatre – and haul myself up the huge steps until I reach the very top with fine views back down to the stage area.

Travelling solo also means that there's no pressure on me to see things either. So, when I visit Florence and notice the massive queues for the duomo snaking around its great girth, I decide I don't want to spend my time standing in line and choose to visit the much quieter Palazzo Vecchio instead where I spend a good deal of time in the map room.

I just know that people are going to ask if I climbed Brunelleschi's dome or saw the famous Uffizi Gallery and the Galleria dell'Accademia, and I'm very lucky that I have seen all these on my highlights trip in 1994. But you should never feel pressure to visit places unless there is a true passion to do so. My return trip to Florence is about just wandering. Although I do want to indulge myself in a movie moment. The Loggia della Signoria was covered in scaffolding on my first visit so I couldn't sit there like Helena Bonham Carter did in the film *A Room with a View*. But I can this time and, as I sit taking in the statues and the glorious buildings around the piazza, it occurs to me that, while I first came to Florence as Lucy Honeychurch, I have returned thirty years later as Eleanor Lavish.

Later, I cross the Ponte Vecchio. Crowds jostle under a rainbow array of umbrellas and the gold gleaming from the shop windows seems even brighter because of the grey day. There is one display of Botticelli-inspired jewellery which is irresistible – delicate pieces in gold, pink and turquoise. Two blonde beauties from *Primavera* are being used to advertise the pieces, their fifteenth-century faces luminous and beautiful. I look around at the tourists and acknowledge the fact that the Ponte Vecchio has been parting people from their money for over six hundred years.

The third destination of my trip is Padua. The main draw for me here is the Scrovegni Chapel made famous by the extraordinary frescoes depicting the lives of Mary and Jesus, painted by Giotto around 1305. I pass the tiny chapel as I walk into town from the train station, but I'm far too early for my timed slot, so continue on my way. I book myself on an afternoon tour of the Palazzo Bo – the university of Padua – sincerely hoping I make it back there in time after visiting the chapel. In the meantime, I have just enough time to tour the stunning Palazzo Ragione in Piazza delle Erbe.

This is one of the great joys of only having myself to please – I can jumble all of these wonderful arty activities together, one after another – and not have to worry if that's not to somebody else's taste or if my timetable is a little too punishing. Of course, it might well leave me depleted by the end of the day, but at least I won't be answerable to anybody but myself.

The Scrovegni Chapel is approached via an air-controlled room where you watch a ten-minute video before being allowed into the chapel itself. The door is firmly closed behind you. I am the only solo and have joined a group of American tourists. It feels a little odd – as if I have gate-crashed their party – but you have to get used to this sort of thing as a solo traveller. Besides, I have little time to get anxious about it because the frescoes are stunning, as is the heavenly blue ceiling studded with stars.

One of the frescoes depicts what is thought to be the first kiss in art and I soon find it. I see another famous kiss – that given by Judas to Jesus. There's also an extraordinary fresco where Jesus has been taken down from the cross and ten tiny angels hover in the sky above him, their faces etched with grief.

After fifteen minutes, an alarm sounds and we are ushered out the way we came in. I walk quickly back into town and make it in time for my tour of the Palazzo Bo. The tour is being led by a young American student who is in Padua studying for her master's degree in Sustainable Tourism. She is full of enthusiasm, has a lovely bright smile and gives us so much information. We see the podium Galileo taught from, and the dissecting room from the viewpoint of the cadaver, looking up at the staged seating area above.

We're then shown into a room with a large table at its centre which is still very much used today. It's watched over by a row of skulls housed in a glass cabinet. These skulls belong to previous professors who donated themselves to the now defunct study of phrenology and I wonder what it must be like to sit at the table in their company.

After the tour ends, I walk across town to visit the Basilica of St Anthony and then go on to the Prato della Valle – one of the largest squares in Europe, bordered by a statue-studded canal. I have walked miles and have seen so many wonders. It's been a totally indulgent day where I happily ate on the move so that I could see as much as possible, and I've loved every minute of it.

Bologna – My Home for the Week

After three busy days seeing beautiful cities, it's time to explore my base for the week. I'm trying to arrange my timetable so that I have time in Bologna between visiting other places which should give me time to relax on the mornings when I don't have to rush to the train station.

One thing I've been really looking forward to seeing in Bologna is the Basilica of San Luca which sits on a hill outside the city. I catch the San Luca Express road train which picks up tourists from the Piazza Maggiore and winds its way through the streets and into the hills with views across the glorious countryside of Emilia-Romagna. The train has just three carriages and, as I get inside, I say hello, in Italian, to a couple already inside. I quickly realise they're English. Their names are Colin and Caroline and we swap notes about our experience of Bologna and walk up to the church together when we get off the train. We are going to climb the tower.

It's windy at the top and, almost immediately, Colin's cap blows right off his head and lands on the beautiful terracotta tiles far below. There's no way of retrieving it and we see that it's joined a small handbag already there.

'It'll be a great story to tell the folks back home,' I say as we take photos for each other with the view back to the city of Bologna behind us. It looks beautiful from here and you can see why it's been given one of its nicknames: *La Rossa* – The Red – because the buildings are a wonderful warm red in the midst of the green landscape.

Another place I want to see is the *Archiginnasio* which was once the main building of the University of Bologna – the oldest university in Europe. It's just three euros to enter and the corridors alone are worth the money. The Anatomical Theatre with two carved wooden figures known as 'The Skinned' is like nothing I've ever seen before. I spend a bit of time admiring it all although I try not to speculate what has been examined in the past on the white marble table in the centre of this great wooden room.

But the room that leaves me completely breathless is the Municipal Library. Visitors can only see it through a metal barrier but I take a good long sniff and think that my *Book Lovers* cast would do

exactly the same thing. Housing 850,000 books, it reminds me of something from an Indiana Jones film. The visitor's view is funnelled through two rows of glass-fronted bookcases towards the doorway into the first section, which leads to another and another and another: an enfilade of knowledge which seems to stretch to infinity. It's so very tantalising and I long to walk the length of it.

Bologna is very good at capturing the eye and the imagination. It's famous for its porticoes – the covered walkways with beautiful arches, columns and painted ceilings – and these are most welcome during my rainy stay in the city as I wend my way across town. One of the most stunning is on Farini Street and I manage to find it, struggling with my umbrella as I tuck its damp folds under my arm and crane my head back to photograph the gilded scenes above me. It's busy here and I'm struggling a little with the crowds so I quickly move on, stuffing in an ear plug and turning the noise of the world down by fifty percent. For an introvert used to life in a country village, ear plugs truly are an essential travel companion, making cities bearable and allowing me to be out in the full jostle of life without completely depleting myself.

Trains, Rain and Feeling the Strain

It's just a half hour train ride from Bologna to the city of Ferrara. I have my ticket but I see that I must validate it and can't work out where to do this. I march up and down the platform and don't see any machines. Is it a deal breaker? Will I be thrown off the train or charged extra? I really don't know. Still, it makes the short train ride a little bit nerve-wracking.

I choose an upstairs seat, enjoying the sensation of viewing the landscape from above. It's so much fun. The trouble is, I need to use the toilet before I get off and that's all the way at the back of the train and it takes me a little while to get there. When I come out, I decide to sit downstairs. Ferrara is only a couple of minutes away now and it's when the station is announced that I see a ticket officer approaching. In fact, he's just a few seats in front of me. I'm sure I have done absolutely nothing wrong by not validating my ticket as I've paid for it in full, but I'm anxious that I'm about to be told off or even fined, so I casually get up and make my way towards the doors where there are other passengers standing in preparation to disembark. I feel like a fugitive, but I make it off the train without incident.

Ferrara is another destination where I'm not sure how to get into town or how far the city centre actually is. After a bit of faffing around, which I'm getting quite good at by now, I discover there's a bus and get on board. The driver, a surly woman, tells me to scan my card. She then gets off and I'm left completely alone which is just as well because I soon realise I'm trying to scan my card at an old coin machine. The one I should be using is further along the bus. Thank goodness nobody witnessed this particular gaffe, I think.

The journey into town is a straightforward one, with the bus dropping me off right outside the moated Castle Estense, and I decide to walk back to the station at the end of my day here as even I can't mess that route up. But this is one of the things I enjoy most about solo travelling – although *enjoy* isn't perhaps quite the right word. So much of the time is spent problem-solving: little things like buying a train or bus ticket and working out how to get to a museum across town. In the moment, it can seem stressful and overwhelming. There is nobody by your side to help you or back you up. But the sense of achievement – and relief – when you get something right, and the surge of confidence that follows is heartening and rather addictive. And the rewards are always worth the stress.

As I walk down the cobbled medieval street of the Via delleVolte, I can feel myself relaxing. This is what it's all about for me – finding these beautiful places and moments. I take a few pictures, aware of the young man with a very serious looking camera in front of me. We both do a strange dance trying to get out of each other's shots. We are chasing the same images and don't want each other spoiling them.

There is one more test I face in Ferrara. I've found a lovely pizzeria overlooking the back of the castle and take a seat and look around for a menu. There isn't one. A moment later, a waitress drops a tiny card on my table – a card with a dreaded QR code on it. I obviously look helpless because she takes pity on me and helps me find the restaurant's menu on my phone, but I don't like having to click and scroll back and forth trying to hold the information in my head and not being able to see everything at once. The QR codes are something I'm going to have to get friendly with as they seem to be following me all over Europe.

Another trip filled with a series of challenges is when I attempt to get myself to Mantua. I'm catching the 8.33 a.m. train and I'm extremely nervous because I have to change trains in Modena and there are just eight minutes in which to do that. *Eight minutes.* With the best will in the world, navigating a new station with early morning commuters is going to be tricky. But it becomes even trickier when, even though my train leaves Bologna on time, it promptly stops outside the city for a full ten minutes. I message Roy on WhatsApp and he tries to keep me calm by saying that perhaps the Mantua train will be running late as well. But I have no such luck and miss my connection.

I speak to a young man at the ticket office who, luckily, speaks wonderful English and who offers to refund me, but tells me there is another train – in three hours. That doesn't really give me enough time in Mantua and I really don't fancy a three-hour wait at a noisy station. So I decide to spend the day in Modena and he gives me a partial refund on my ticket.

'I'm trying to think of somewhere else for you go to,' he tells me.

'Oh, I'll stay here in Modena,' I tell him. It's very kind of him to care, but I'm already here and I've done a little research about the city in case my connecting train didn't work out.

I walk into town as it seems quite straightforward from Google Maps. The sun is shining and I'm determined to make the best of things, although I can't help mourning Mantua a little because I did so much research into it, but perhaps I'm meant to see Modena instead.

However, when I try to visit the tower in the centre of town and realise that you have to book using a QR code, I nearly lose my patience. I manage to scan the code and start entering all the requested details, but then it asks for my phone number. I sigh. I still don't actually know it by heart and so I give up. But, a few minutes later, as I enter the cathedral, I think of the hours that lie ahead of me in this town that I'm not overly prepared for today and I decide to conquer this QR business. I find a pew and fish out the little post-it note from my wallet on which I've handwritten my phone number. A few seconds later, I've managed to book a slot at noon to climb the tower and I can't help feeling just a little bit proud of myself. And it's definitely worth the effort because, although it's a long way up, the steps are wide and shallow so it's fairly easy going.

Being inside the tower is rather like inhabiting an M C Escher drawing with the steps, arches and enormous central drop. It takes my mind off having missed Mantua today, and I can't help but wonder if I was meant to see all this instead.

The next testing train trip is on my final day of exploration. I bought a return ticket to Parma earlier in the week, but the torrential rain this morning has caused chaos on the railways and my train is running half an hour late. A few minutes later, a forty-minute delay is announced and I see that the Parma train before mine has been cancelled. At least mine is still scheduled and is leaving from the same platform – platform three – so I stay put.

I message Roy and he tells me there is dreadful flooding in Europe in the wake of Storm Boris. There have been over twenty fatalities. Places along the Danube like Vienna, Bratislava and Budapest are affected – places I visited on my last solo trip. And the weather is heading to the very region I'm in. A yellow alert has been issued with warnings of storms, landslides and floods, and the Emilia-Romagna and Marche areas are of the greatest concern with

the region under threat of two months' worth of rainfall in the next three days. Roy advises that it's probably best not to travel today.

I think of all the things that could go wrong and I think about spending one of my precious days locked away – albeit safely – in my bed and breakfast room. Then, from the corner of my eye, I see a man slipping and falling as he runs for a train across the wet platform. I go to help as does another commuter, and the fallen man gets to his feet. He hobbles away, clearly hurt and distressed, and the incident puts me on edge. Should I go back to my B&B? I don't really want to spend a day in my room and the streets of Bologna will be as dangerous – if not more so – than Parma. But what if I make it to my destination and then can't get back?

I'm really panicking now and look at the departures board again. There's been a huge leap in the delay to my train's departure time to ninety-five minutes. I'm finding it hard to work out when it's actually due now as the new time of departure hasn't been put on the board – you have to work it out for yourself. I watch the board for a few moments and then ask a nearby woman in a ticket booth.

'Your train is the next to leave from platform seven,' she says.

Suddenly, after waiting for so long at my original platform, my train is departing from a different one and I have to run to catch it. But at least I'm now on my way to Parma.

Why on earth am I putting myself through all this, I can't help asking as I glance out of the rain-streaked window of the train? When I pose the question to Aussie Vicki via WhatsApp, she comes back with a sage reply.

'What doesn't kill you makes you a better solo traveller!'

And the thing is – no matter what the stress of the journey might be – I always feel as if it's worth it. Parma is a true highlight of my trip and I fall in love with the pink Verona marble of the Baptistery and the beautiful carvings of fantastical creatures all the way around it. Even though I have to photograph it from underneath my umbrella, I'm so grateful to have been able to see it, and I make it safely back to my bed and breakfast later that day.

Don't Stand Still For Too Long

There's a lesson I quickly learn during my solo trip to Italy and it's that I'm at my most vulnerable when standing still. The first time I realise this is when I'm buying train tickets at the station in Florence. My train back to Bologna is forty minutes late and I've arrived at the station forty minutes before my train was originally scheduled to leave, so I have a long time to fill. I decide to get organised for the rest of the week, booking tickets for three more day trips and I do this using the machines as they are pretty straightforward.

Alas, I get approached twice while trying to get my tickets sorted – including by a young man who asks for fifty euro cents. It seems like an odd amount to ask for and I immediately think he's after my wallet and will grab that if I dare to take it out to give him the small coin he's asking for. I've been warned about beggars approaching while using the ticket machines and I simply shake my head and refuse to engage. But it does make me wary.

I'm also on my guard every time I stop to consult Google Maps on my phone in the street. It's particularly trying in Bologna where I'm approached countless times by street sellers doing their best to sell umbrellas, but it's very unnerving when they approach from behind because you fear they're about to try and grab your bag or phone.

One incident that surprises me is when I'm closing my umbrella outside a church in Parma and a beggar asks for money. I try not to engage and walk inside the church, but he follows me in, telling me he's had nothing but crackers to eat for two days. I give him a couple of euros and he gives me a filthy look as if expecting more.

This isn't the only time I'm followed into a church. As I'm about to enter the Church of Corpus Domini in Bologna, I'm temporarily stopped in my tracks when the entrance appears to be roped off. There's a man mopping the floor just inside but I can't catch his eye. It's as I'm pondering what to do that a guy in his thirties approaches me from the street.

'Are you going inside?' he asks in English.

'I'm not sure the church is open,' I say.

The guy immediately takes control of things, calling to the man with the mop and then guiding me into the church.

'I saw you and thought I'd come in,' he tells me.

I'm a little anxious about this admission, but he seems friendly enough and I'm grateful that he's managed to get me inside. I've had a long walk to get here and there's something very particular I'm hoping to see: St Catherine of Bologna. Born in 1413, she died in 1463 and her mummified body is on display in the church, sitting upright in a chair, her hands clasped together in prayer.

'Have you seen the saint before?' I ask my companion now as we walk to the front of the church.

'A long time ago when I was a little boy.'

He has a rather wild sort of energy and I wonder if, perhaps, there are chemicals sloshing around his system. He starts telling me how much he loves England and how he's been to Devon and Wales.

'And Bristol!' he says excitedly. I try not to laugh at his enthusiasm.

As we reach the front of the church, I see a big screen to the left of the nave with a round window cut into it through which you can clearly see the centuries-darkened skin of Saint Catherine's face. It's a weird sensation knowing she's over five hundred years old.

My companion crosses himself and encourages me to do the same.

'You got to be careful with this shit!' he says.

I bite my lip as he isn't exactly whispering and there's a woman at prayer behind us. I'm pretty certain you shouldn't be swearing in front of a saint.

We spend a little time looking at her and then he asks me a question.

'Can I buy you a drink?'

'No, thank you.'

'Are you married?' He strokes my arm. 'Is this cashmere? It's so soft!'

I'm so surprised that I don't think I say anything.

'Walk with me into town,' he goes on.

'No. I'm staying here.'

I feel as if I need the saint's protection.

He says goodbye, still smiling and I watch him go, relief filling me. This sort of attention is definitely one of the downsides of travelling solo.

But there is one time when I reach out to a local man quite early in my trip. It's when I'm trying to get back to the train station in

Padua. I've walked miles and I'm tired and I'm hoping someone can tell me where to catch the tram or bus. I pluck up my courage and, in my best Italian — which is very limited — ask a man who looks like he could be a local. His name is Renato and he doesn't speak a single word of English. He insists that it's only a ten-minute walk to the train station, but I know it's closer to half an hour. Still, I decide to go with him as he leads the way. It'll be nice to have his company and he quickly proves to be a wonderful guide, seeing me safely across roads and pointing out a canal view at the Ponte delle Torricelle. He also makes sure I see the Piazza dei Signori and a statue of some kind of creature on a plinth which I'd missed earlier. It looks very old, but I can't understand what he's telling me about it.

I manage to ask a few questions and when I tell him my name he smiles.

'Regina Vittoria,' he declares.

I tell him where I'm from and where I am staying, and the places I hope to visit, and it's a poignant moment when we finally reach the long straight road that will lead me to the train station. It's time to say goodbye and we shake hands and I thank him profusely.

For all the wonderful art and architecture I've seen in Padua, it's moments like this that make a place truly memorable.

Scatty Tax

I can hardly believe that Italy is my fifth solo trip. When I started my tentative travels last year, I had no idea that I'd grow so much in confidence and be able to navigate my way around so many exciting places. But I have to confess to making a few mistakes along the way. It would be hard not to, I guess, and I'm learning to accept that each trip will be testing in some way.

I've made peace with the fact that, sometimes, I'll need to spend an extra bit of money – or energy – trying to work something out on my own. I call this my Scatty Tax.

The first payment of my Scatty Tax on my Italian trip is when I attempt to use the safe in my room. It's placed inside the wardrobe and looks like the one I had in Crete. Being ultra careful, I determine to test it out while it's empty. I try to set a code, pressing the hashtag but not really knowing what I'm doing. Do people intuitively know this stuff? Why aren't there instructions?

I try again and again and the safe finally locks. But, when I try to open it, it doesn't work and I'm not sure what I've done. It's only a few seconds later that I see a piece of paper in a wooden bowl inside the wardrobe. It's the instructions to the safe.

I WhatsApp Roy and Aussie Vicki. I can't be the first person in the world to have done this, but I'm fearful of being given a hefty fine if they have to bring in a locksmith. Roy sends me a few possible overriding codes which might work, but they don't, alas. Aussie Vicki tells me, 'It's no biggie'. She's walked into hotels where the safe was already locked and the staff just come and work their magic.

'Relax, there's always a work around,' she tells me which is great all-round advice.

My first monetary payment of my Scatty Tax happens on my first evening in Bologna. I've been exploring for a couple of hours, drifting happily around the streets, but when I attempt to walk back to my accommodation, I discover that Google Maps has sent me in completely the wrong direction. I'm exhausted after my travel day and so walk into the nearest shop to ask directions. Alas, the young man behind the counter doesn't speak English and escorts me outside where he calls to his neighbour – a lady who is just locking her shop up for the night. The two of them examine the map on my phone and I repeat the name of the road I'm staying on, but they're having trouble communicating in English and point me to a bar along the street.

'He speaks English,' the woman tells me. I thank them and the man in the bar confirms that I am, indeed, walking in completely the wrong direction. As I retrace my steps, I can't help feeling so grateful to these kind people for helping me. I feel like I have three new allies and have had a little insight into this community of shop owners in Bologna.

It's a few minutes later when I spot a taxi dropping somebody off and I decide to grab it. I'm exhausted and I'm still not sure how to get back. As we drive, I chat to the taxi driver, saying how warm it is compared to the UK.

'It's twenty-six degrees,' he tells me. No wonder I was struggling.

It's exasperating not being able to find my own way back, but the money I saved getting the bus from the airport is now spent on a taxi back to my bed and breakfast so it all balances out. It's hard to get everything right when you travel solo and I feel as if I've done pretty well to get myself all the way to Bologna on my own. The taxi ride is a small price to pay for such independence.

That night in Bologna isn't the only time I panic grab a taxi. After managing to catch the bus from the train station into the centre of Verona and thus knowing how to find my way back again, I decide to get super organised and go into a tabacchi shop to buy a ticket for the bus. It takes a little of the pressure off my return journey as I won't have to worry about ticket machines or surly drivers. I am ready.

I allow a full hour to get back to the train station but, after waiting over half an hour, I'm getting decidedly anxious. I look around and spot a taxi rank. I'm annoyed because I've already paid for my bus ticket but how long do I give it? I don't even know if one is on its way and I can't risk missing my train as the ticket was expensive and I'm not sure if I'm allowed to travel at any other than the printed time.

I make my decision and run towards the taxi rank, getting in one after a couple of tourists get out. It costs me €10 but it's worth it because I make my train in plenty of time.

I'm slowly learning to forgive myself when I make mistakes or if I end up spending a little extra money for peace of mind or personal safety. Unpredictable moments are all part of the travel experience and – as in life – we can only respond to them with good humour while remembering that they often make for the best stories to tell our friends and family when we get back home.

Self-Care for Introverts in a City

My nine-night stay in Bologna has been brilliant and exhausting in equal measure. Being based in a city and spending virtually every day visiting other cities on public transport has been exhausting. The constant stimuli and noise from people and traffic is challenging for someone who lives in the countryside, and navigating and working things out on my own is a real test of patience and perseverance.

Here are some tips for surviving city life as an introvert:

Eat well. Take time to sit and really enjoy your food. Find a quiet café or restaurant, ideally one without loud music or lots of children. But make no apologies for retreating to your accommodation with a supermarket sandwich if you need to!

Exercise. Inevitably, you will be walking a lot so make sure you train way ahead for your trip. I always take my travelling yoga mat with me and make time for a quiet, meditative practice. It helps keep me supple and calm.

Find green spaces. Parks, botanical gardens or just a tree with a shady spot to sit for a while. Green spaces always energise me and leave me feeling serene and refreshed.

Find a church. There are many small ones which you will often get to yourself. These are perfect sanctuaries from the chaos of city life. Just make sure nobody follows you into them!

Make contact. If you're feeling a little lonely, use your evenings to contact friends and family back home. I love sending photos via WhatsApp. It's a lovely way to share your trip and remember the highlights of each day yourself.

Rest. When I get back to my accommodation, I make a comfy little nest of cushions on the bed and rest my travel-weary legs. I also listen to music or an audiobook, read or journal. I always take a few herbal tea bags with me so I can enjoy a warm drink. I've found most places either don't leave any tea or it's all caffeinated so I go prepared.

Sleep. Get plenty! I go to bed much earlier when I'm away from home and set my alarm clock earlier too because I want to make the very best of my time away.

Lessons Learned in Italy

•Don't judge the whole of your trip after a travel day and the chaos of arriving in a strange place.

•Don't judge a city on its outskirts, roundabouts or train stations!

•Don't write off a trip in moments of panic. When I arrived at Bologna Centrale, I was chanting, *'Never again! It's too hard! I can't do it!'* But I persevered and had a wonderful trip that I'll never forget.

•Pace yourself. I did my best to arrange my timetable so that I wasn't doing too many long train journeys one after another. It's very easy to overdo things when you want to make the most of your time away.

•Be kind to yourself. If you're feeling exhausted and can't face a walk back to the train station or your accommodation, hop in a taxi and make no apologies for doing so. This is your trip so do it your way.

Reflections on a Year of Solo Adventures

When I look back on this year, I still can't quite believe I've seen so many beautiful places – and that I got to them by myself. I've certainly come a long way since that first flight I took with my friend Rosie last year after neither of us had been abroad for fifteen years.

Did I really find my way to Budapest and walk along the banks of the Danube? Was that really me crossing the Bosphorus on my own that night in a taxi and wending my way through the Grand Bazaar in Istanbul? Did I really find the courage to fling myself off a mountain and paraglide down to the sea in Tenerife? And was it *me* who arranged flights and accommodation, researched new cities and worked out exciting itineraries before navigating my way around on buses, trams, boats and trains? I still can hardly believe it.

I've taken four very different solo trips this year: the first to Tenerife was a package deal where I booked the flight and hotel together; the second to Turkey was with G Adventures where I travelled with a group but also added a few days solo at the end; the third was my most adventurous: travelling between three countries (Austria, Slovakia and Hungary) by public transport; and the fourth to northern Italy was where I based myself in Bologna while exploring other cities by train.

There were elements of each which I loved. I adored the freedom of choice I had when I was on my own, like being able to do exactly what I wanted, for instance taking *The Sound of Music* tour in Salzburg which would send my husband running for the hills – and not in song, I hasten to add! Or spending hours in a wonderful museum late into the evening as I did in Vienna or taking an afternoon off in my hotel in Budapest because it was raining and I was tired and just wanted to have a swim and a nap.

Equally, I loved making new friends on the G Adventures tour. Sharing confidences with Carla after a Turkish massage, and sitting in the theatre at Hierapolis with Ella, Amanda and Jill were special moments I'll always cherish. But being solo could also put a lot of pressure on me and be exhausting – especially if something went wrong.

I have yet to feel that a trip has been a perfect fit. My hotel in Tenerife was definitely much too big and noisy for me. My Austrian trip was a tad too long – I was seriously flagging by the time I reached Budapest – and I was definitely missing green spaces during my city-centred Italian trip. But I regret none of them because I saw and learned so much – not just about the world but about myself. Each trip taught me something wonderful, gave me confidence and proved that I could cope with so many things that used to terrify me.

Everything still terrifies me, by the way. I'll always have those anxiety dreams in the run-up to a trip, worrying about how to navigate an airport or how I'm going to find my accommodation. I think I'll always have butterflies in my stomach before leaving my accommodation each morning and I'll forever be anxious that I'm heading the wrong way in a new city, and that the bus or train I've just caught is actually going the way I hope it's going.

Some people believe that travel is an escape and, in some ways, it is for me too. But I think it's much more a moving *towards* life rather than an escape from it – a move towards something vital. It's a way of living in the moment and feeling totally alive. It's about waking up in the morning and wondering what exciting new things you're going to see and experience. It's about making time for yourself. Time to see, to hear, to engage all the senses, and to walk through places you've never walked through before and to connect with new people and share special moments.

I don't want to sound too dramatic but my year of solo trips has been both revolutionary and revelatory. I've learned so much and *lived* so much. It's been exhausting and exciting, terrifying and stimulating. And I can't wait to do it all again next year!

Join Victoria on her Travels!

Did you know that Victoria now has a YouTube channel?
Join her at **EnglishWriterExplores** to find out more about some of the places she's been visiting recently.

youtube.com/@englishwriterexplores

Also by Victoria Connelly

The House in the Clouds Series

The House in the Clouds
High Blue Sky
The Colour of Summer

The Book Lovers Series

The Book Lovers
Rules for a Successful Book Club
Natural Born Readers
Scenes from a Country Bookshop
One More Page Before I Kiss You
Christmas with the Book Lovers

Other Books

Family Portrait
The Way to the Sea
The Beauty of Broken Things
One Last Summer
The Heart of the Garden
Love in an English Garden

The Rose Girls
The Secret of You
The Wrong Ghost
Christmas at The Cove
Christmas at the Castle
Christmas at the Cottage
A Summer to Remember
Wish You Were Here
The Runaway Actress
Molly's Millions
Flights of Angels
Irresistible You
Three Graces
A Weekend with Mr Darcy
The Perfect Hero (Dreaming of Mr Darcy)
Mr Darcy Forever
Christmas With Mr Darcy
Happy Birthday Mr Darcy
At Home with Mr Darcy
Escape to Mulberry Cottage (non-fiction)
A Year at Mulberry Cottage (non-fiction)
Summer at Mulberry Cottage (non-fiction)
Finding Old Thatch (non-fiction)
The Garden at Old Thatch (non-fiction)

About the Author

Victoria Connelly is the bestselling author of *The Rose Girls* and *The Book Lovers* series.

With over a million sales, her books have been translated into many languages. The first, *Flights of Angels*, was made into a film in Germany. Victoria flew to Berlin to see it being made and even played a cameo role in it.

A Weekend with Mr Darcy, the first in her popular Austen Addicts series about fans of Jane Austen has sold over 100,000 copies. She is also the author of several romantic comedies including *The Runaway Actress* which was nominated for the Romantic Novelists' Association's Best Romantic Comedy of the Year.

Victoria was brought up in Norfolk, England before moving to Yorkshire where she got married in a medieval castle. After 11 years in London, she moved to rural Suffolk where she lives in a pink thatched cottage with her artist husband, a springer spaniel and her ex-battery hens.

To hear about future releases and receive a **free ebook** sign up for her newsletter at www.victoriaconnelly.com.

Sometimes, it's those closest to you who are hiding the most.

After the death of their artist father, Alex, Brenna and Cordelia Bellwood return to Slate House – the Victorian mansion in the Lake District where they grew up together. But the three siblings have very different memories of being there and of their relationship with their famous father.

For Alex, his passion for art was always overshadowed by his father's fame. For Brenna, life was turned upside down when their mother left them, forcing her to grow up much too quickly. And Cordelia – once the beloved muse of her father – now questions her role after a shocking revelation that threatens the whole family.

Set against the beautiful backdrop of Grasmere, *Family Portrait* is a lyrical and poignant story showing that the things that tear us apart can also bring us together again.

MILLION SELLING AUTHOR

VICTORIA CONNELLY

FAMILY PORTRAIT

Author Victoria Connelly hasn't been abroad for fifteen years, but a sudden longing to see the world hits her hard and she decides it's time to venture forth from her peaceful country cottage.

But what's it like travelling as an introvert who's battling menopause, chronic nerves and Google Maps?

Join Victoria as she visits Amsterdam with a friend, Sicily with her brother, Belgium with her husband and Crete – on her own!

With over 20 colour photos, Introvert Abroad is a delightful memoir full of inspiration and humour, proving introverts everywhere can feel the fear and travel anyway.

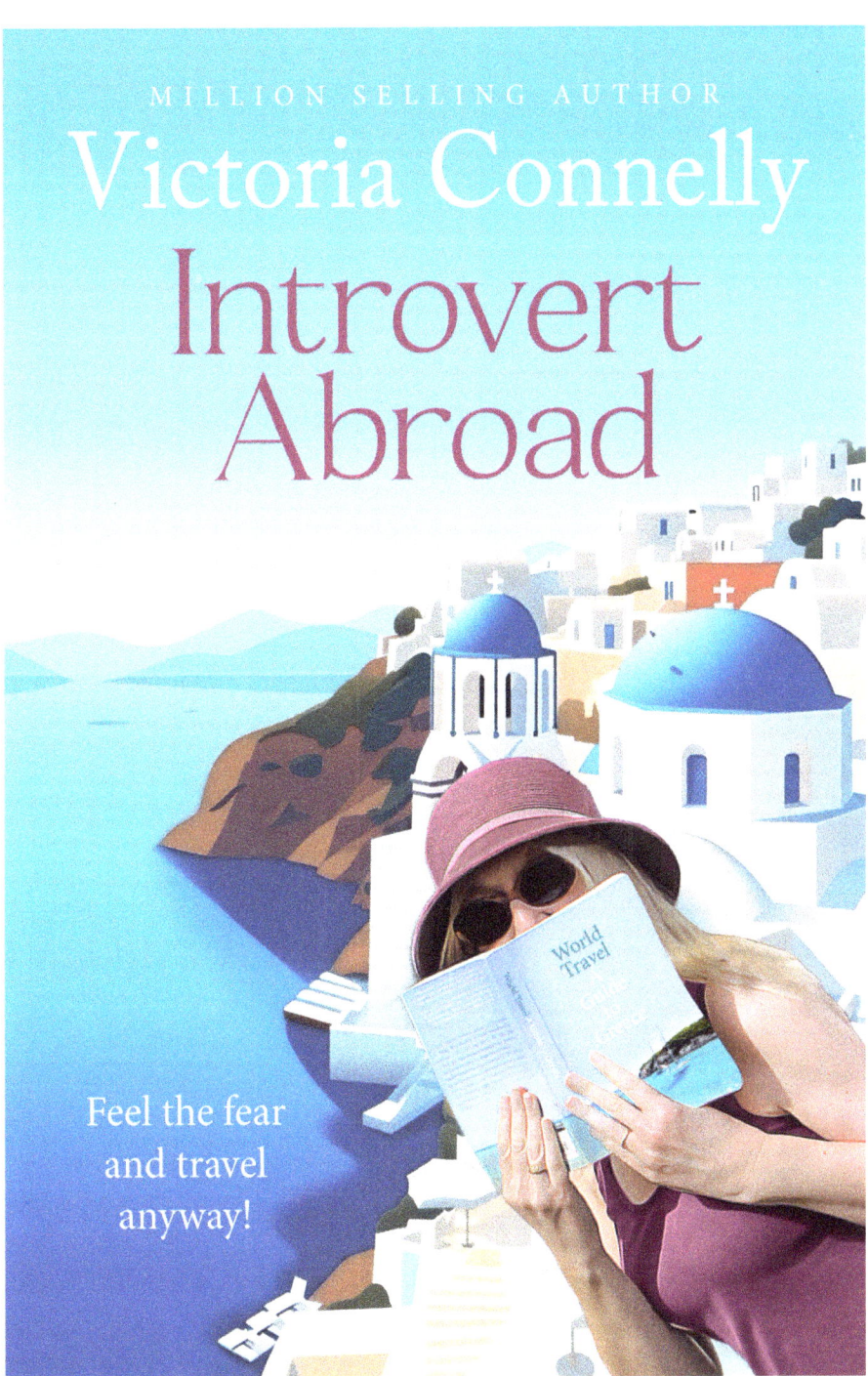

www.ingramcontent.com/pod-product-compliance
Lightning Source LLC
Chambersburg PA
CBHW061231070526
44584CB00030B/4083